Advance praise for Coyote Woman . . .

"Tina's blend of honesty, intuition, and mysticism is a unique experience and one that should be had by all."

—Mark Bryan
Coauthor of *The Artist's Way at Work: Riding the Dragon*

"Seldom are precision and lyricism combined in such generous helpings, and yet, added to the delicious beauty and detail of the writing, *Coyote Woman* expresses the spiritual homesickness so many feel today. In describing her return to Santa Fe, Tina Le Marque illumines the path Home."

—Hugh Prather and Gayle Prather
Authors of *Notes to Each Other* and *Spiritual Notes to Myself*

Also by Tina Le Marque

Warrior Woman: A Journal of My Life As an Artist

COYOTE WOMAN

COYOTE WOMAN

A CONTINUING JOURNAL OF MY LIFE AS AN ARTIST

TINA LE MARQUE

ARTISTS AND WRITERS PRESS
SANTA FE, NEW MEXICO

Published by: Artists and Writers Press
223 North Guadalupe Street, Suite #303
Santa Fe, NM 87505

Editor: Ellen Kleiner
Book design and typography: Richard Harris
Cover design: Tina Le Marque
Cover production: Janice St. Marie
Front cover photograph: Ford Robbins
Back cover photograph: Daniel Nadelbach; make-up by Gilda Meyer-Niehof
Index: Kate Bowman

A Blessingway book

Publisher's Cataloging-in-Publication Data

Le Marque, Tina, 1951–
Coyote woman : a continuing journal of my life as an artist / Tina Le Marque. — 1st ed.
p. cm.
Preassigned LCCN: 97-72381
ISBN: 0-9630131-1-4

1. Le Marque, Tina, 1951– —Diaries. 2. Painters—United States —Diaries. 3. Feminism and art—United States. I. Title

ND237.L39A2 1998 759.13 [B]
QBI97-41228

Printed in the United States of America on acid-free recycled paper

10 9 8 7 6 5 4 3 2 1

This book is dedicated to the strong women and all of us who are on our way . . .

To Naomi, the woman I most want to be like when I grow up, and Alex, an orchid, not a daisy

To the Dorothys—Dorothy Cannon, Dorothy Royer, and especially my mother, Dorothy June

To the "women who know too much" of the Sonoran Desert—Janee, Frances, Deb, Karen, Margaret, Laurie, Glenda, Lis, Patti, Jean Marie

To Heidi and Meigen, my cactus flowers

And most of all to the woman who fished me out of the plumbing, dried me off, fluffed me up, and brought me back to life—Jeanne Johnson Theodore.

So far, so good.

In gratitude . . .

Ellen Kleiner, I couldn't have faced the past without you. And Bob D., I love you like a river, like the mountain, like the sky.

About Coyote Woman . . .

For a period of about two years I was involved in a hot quest to paint a recurring character from my own mythology whom I came to know as Coyote Woman. Coyote Woman represents all that is unknown in life, coupled with the tendency for unexpected events to pop up in the middle of situations that seem neatly resolved. Coyote Woman is the embodiment of Fool energy as it manifests in the realm of the feminine.

Over the course of writing this book, I painted a half dozen renditions of this character, all different from one another. In the beginning of my quest to put Coyote Woman onto canvas, she was very much human in form. As successive paintings emerged, she became less human, more archetypal. The image intensified with each attempt until the painting that graces the cover of this book was accomplished. This painting is imbued with the power and mystery that is embodied in my ally and teacher, the great trickster, Coyote Woman.

Contents

Foreword

Invisible Things Spoken, Shown

As a professor of Writing Studies, I have thought long and hard about the ingredients of good writing. What is it that makes someone's words engaging, inspirational, momentous? How does Toni Morrison, for example, give me hope even though most of her characters' lives overflow with a despair more profound than I could ever imagine, much less endure? How does Louise Erdrich create men and women of such dignity in landscapes so dilapidated and with words so sparse? How does bell hooks move me to tears even though she writes in the off-putting and impenetrable language of academic discourse?

I also often think about the process of writing, about the strategies and habits that make good writers artists as well as technicians. As a writer myself, I know how frustrating it is to try to learn a process that is so private, so esoteric, so unwieldy. As a writing teacher, I know how impossibly difficult it is to teach such an intractable course. In fact, because so little of the act of writing is visible, because following our own minds' habits as we create meaning is exhausting and time-consuming, because writing—like any other art—requires so much courage, we mystify the process. We get impatient with the long, slow slope of writing's learning curve and conclude in exasperation, "Either you're born with it or you're not, and if you're not, there's not much else you can do about it." This mystification somehow excuses us from the commitment and discipline it takes to learn to write well; it's how we abdicate the courage to create.

And rest assured that if you don't believe it takes great courage to create, any brief foray into a creative activity will convince you of this truth. Rollo May knew it; so did Ann Sexton. Taped to my computer is my favorite of her sayings:

> I think that writers must try not to avoid knowing what is happening. Everyone has somewhere the ability to mask the events of pain and sorrow. But the creative person must not use this mechanism any more than they have to in order to keep breathing.

That, I think, is much of what good writing is—a gathering of someone's mindful observations, someone who's drenched in what is happening, baptized in the events of pain and sorrow, grief and despair, ecstasy and elation, and most especially, passion and creation.

But—as you surely know—not all writing is good, not all writers are mindful in their observations, and some observers are unwilling to cogently gather what they've recognized and lived. As an academic writer and teacher, I have seen far too many writers desperately avoid knowing what's happening, masking the events of pain and sorrow with Reason and Expertise. And though I have tried to introduce passion and particulars into the abstract writing of the academy, I must admit that I myself have written some pretty hollow and unfeeling texts; I've even instructed others to do the same.

Not so with Tina Le Marque. Tina has instructed me in how to be just as full and free and feeling as she is. Once, during the most confusing and painful stages of what ultimately became a divorce, I sought refuge in the solitude and beauty of Tina and Bob's desert preserve. Writing to me from someone else's high-desert preserve in Santa Fe, New Mexico, Tina said this: "It's okay to grow and expand, my friend; God won't put you back in a box. God's for freedom. Just look at me."

And look at her I do. What I see is that Tina's an artist first and foremost, a creative person who uses any medium—paint, brushes, words, canvas, photography, music, sticks, stones, a cactus pad, for god's sake, if that's the only thing handy. She'll do whatever it takes to express all of the ephemeral and enduring, enigmatic and obvious, ineffable and ordinary experience and emotion that constitute being the woman she is: a daughter, a mother, a sister, a niece; a painter, dancer, teacher, writer; an alcoholic, a sponsor and a sponsee, a speaker of renown, and an ordinary sister among many; a wife, an ex-wife, a vamp, and a shrew; a spiritual seeker and pathfinder, a kid and a crone; a warrior of the heart and a mess of nerves.

In short, she's someone just like you and someone totally peerless. She's a mystery, and the longer you know her, the more it's true. You'll never be able to capture just who she is, for by the time you think you've pinned her down she's slipped from your grasp like tiny spheres of mercury scurrying along to another corner. And yet she's willing to show herself to you over and over, inside and out; she'll stage for you the process of being the woman she is. And when you look at her, you will certainly see how willing she is *not* to mask the events of pain and sorrow any more than is necessary for her to keep breathing.

And that, I think, is the signature of not just a good writer but a good teacher as well, someone who shows me what she does rather than tells me what I should do. A good teacher of any creative process—be it writing or painting or staying sober or finding a god—is someone who demystifies the process of creating, who is willing to cast off the wizard's smoke, mirroring and laying bare to all of us the person behind the curtain.

In this second gathering of her mindful observations, you'll be witness once again to Tina's passion and creation. She'll show you how she and you, too, can be a human of strength and dignity and laughter; she'll affirm you because you already are.

Jane E. Hindman
San Diego State University

By way of introduction . . .

The sun rose red and wild over the Sangre de Cristo Mountains this December morning, a vivid resurrection after last night's lunar eclipse. Dawn finds me at my desk looking out onto an expanse of cold high desert. Rabbits in bushy winter coats are crouched under cars parked out on the plains. The frost has come and gone, but will return with a vengeance soon and will last for many months.

A little Santa Fe adobe has been my home for six days. At night I burn a fire of cedar and oak. Day and night I watch the sky, reading every nuance for changes in the mood of the desert. Unsuspecting people come out here and find they cannot leave; the astonishing bigness of the sky takes them by surprise and holds them fast. People of spirit find it hard to put themselves back in a box after a sojourn in this open land where the curvilinear landscape creates an inescapable rapture of the deep. New Mexico was once my home, and against all obstacles it has contrived to bring me back.

Seven years ago, in 1986, I flew from my home in Los Angeles to Santa Fe for lunch with an admirer named Bob. Thinking I was coming for only a day, I had no idea that my happy and orderly life was about to be struck by lightning. It was the red dirt of New Mexico that first seduced me; I have always been taken by great beauty. On the way to Santa Fe from the Albuquerque airport, Bob and I had to pull over so I could lie on the earth. Then after a lover's chase that lasted nearly a year, I surrendered and came to the high desert to live, pregnant with our first and only child, whom we named Alexandra, though for many years she called herself Sasha. Bob and I married at a church in Santa Fe six months before she was born.

In the winter of 1989, just before Sasha's first birthday, we left our Santa Fe home for a weekend trip to Tucson. Our vacation was disrupted, however, by a phone call from my mother in California, asking, "Can you come? Your father's acting strange. I'm scared." Come we did, and the longer our "weekend trip" extended, the more our devastation increased, as my father died, followed shortly by Bob's mother. The result of all this death was near-obliteration of the joyous couple who had been very much in love and ecstatic over the arrival of a beautiful healthy baby.

My mother, who could not be left alone in her grief and failing health, was unable to move to the 7,000-foot altitude of Santa Fe. Thinking that happiness was an "inside job," that it didn't matter where we lived, that we could leave Santa Fe since it was rapidly filling up with Hollywood types—which I suppose we were, too, though we didn't think so at the time—and that we were creative writers and artists who could generate our own excitement, Bob and I took up residence with my mother in a home in the Arizona desert where we could write and paint. But there we experienced more solitude than even I could bear.

The next few years, spent in painful exile in the small rural town of Kingman, revealed that there is little joy to be had living in a hyperconservative community when you are an unconventional egg. We nearly perished from loneliness. Hence, in desperation we moved to Tucson, where we found far more happiness despite my mother's rapidly declining health. Against my will, I loved Tucson. It soon became clear, however, that regardless of the city's beautiful setting and endearing people, my heart steadfastly refused to pull up its roots from the red earth of New Mexico.

Six months after our arrival in Tucson, a new round of dying began. Death overtook my dear four-legged companion of twelve years, an aristocratic German shepherd named Bini; then my mother; followed two days later by my father's old hunting dog, Sue. As grief piled upon grief, Santa Fe felt more and more like the refuge I sorely needed, a home for my heart.

While grieving the deaths that left me without parents I, like an emotional North Star, remained fixed on the vision of returning to New Mexico. For nearly three more years, this infatuation kept me putting one foot in front of the other through some of the most difficult transitions of my life.

Now I am home with my husband and child. I do not know how we survived the last five years, but I do know that as a result of our adversity we were all strengthened. Once again, we are enveloped in the beauty of the land, protected, and somehow closer to God.

At this juncture I am forty-two years old and have spent most of my life as an artist. I started painting, working in clay, and gluing bits of this and that together in a children's workshop given by Dorothy Royer, an inspired art teacher in Los Angeles. I went on to attend her classes when I was five and six years old, then returned to paint with her as a troubled young adult. Dorothy introduced me to the landscape of the interior. She also sent me to my first therapist, Ann Salzman, and to a woman who worked with expressive movement, Jane Manning. In chorus these three women began to awaken within me powerful forces of emotional recovery.

What was I needing to recover from? A life spent with two alcoholic parents who were alternately crazed and inspired, terrifying and nurturing. Simply watching from the sidelines would no doubt have destroyed a fainthearted child, but I participated in the traditional way—hiding bottles, constructing elaborate booby traps in the liquor cabinet, and formulating plans to get my mother away from my father, whom I thought was going to kill her. I finally found my forte: controlling the family through dramatic asthma attacks each time the energy in the house turned lethal. These gasping episodes, although life threatening, managed to stop the fighting.

When Dorothy Royer and I had gone as far as we were meant to, she referred me to another great influence in my life as an artist—Dorothy Cannon, who taught all the little artist children in the San Fernando Valley, as well as gifted and troubled teens, and women who were trying to "find themselves" again. She remained my teacher for more than fourteen years.

The Dorothys, both of whom were unique, powerful women, opened me to the world of art and dreams. Each one in her own way led me to an underground river of images where I found my salvation and, in time, my calling. I recognized then that they were two of my spiritual mothers. I still think of them that way, and wonder what would have become of me if God had not led me to their doors.

I also found deliverance as a writer—an occupation I had been compulsively pursuing ever since I could form words. My early life as a writer was nearly brought to a close by an unfortunate introduction to human treachery. When I was eleven, my nineteen-year-old sister, an incurable snoop, broke into my carefully bolted closet, smashed my locked file with a hammer, and read my diary, which was filled with the sexual musings characteristic of a girl on the cusp of adolescence. Following this violation, my sister embarked on months of insidious blackmail. "Take some money out of Mom's purse for me or I'll tell her about your diary," she would threaten. Oh no, I'd think to myself, anything but that! So invaded was I feeling that I considered abandoning writing in favor of the visual mode of self-expression, which was more opaque, less vulnerable to violation.

Nevertheless, I continued down my path as a writer, albeit in a stealthier manner. I became adept at hiding my work—a practice I heartily recommend to beginning writers. All the while, I was shocked to learn that *many* people surreptitiously read the private renderings of writers, pages onto which they have poured their hearts and souls. Creative people, I discovered, are often oblivious to the toxic fascination of intensely jealous sleuths who may follow them throughout their lives.

As a high school senior in a very small private girls' school in the foothills of west Los Angeles, I studied English with yet another extraordinary teacher, Sandy Bugaj. I had been close to dropping out when she appeared in my life; actually, I had been close to dropping dead, skating wildly on a submerged death wish. Sandy Bugaj had developed a teaching technique she called "Experiential English." And experiential it was—using free association, we would jot down all the words that popped into our heads about the day's assigned theme, then expand the words into phrases, and the phrases into sentences.

Sandy's method opened the floodgates for me. What's more, she validated my feelings and valued everything I brought to her, whether it was a piece of writing or an art project instead, both of which were often presented to her in a torrent of tears.

I will never forget the first piece I turned in, which was to be on the theme of "mother." I wrote about going into the kitchen and finding my mother drinking Scotch out of a bottle she kept hidden under the sink. After reading my composition, Sandy took me aside and began to work with me, gradually turning my writing into a rolling, breathing, dancing entity with a life of its own. She was, coincidentally, the same age as my sister, hence her dedication and friendship counteracted many of the negative effects I experienced at home.

Although I had excellent grades and "all the right stuff," as my senior year drew to a close I had no interest at all in attending college. My "lack of academic initiative" caused a stir at school where, out of a graduating class of forty-two, I was one of two girls who chose not to go on to college.

It was at this crossroads in my life that my mother initiated a quest to relocate my innovative childhood art teacher, Dorothy Royer. At that point Dorothy was recognized as a pioneer in art therapy, and through the veils of my unconscious she brought me to art. Her orientation was spiritual, even mystical, and her background was in Jungian psychology. Together, we would enter the caverns of the psyche to uncover images for my paintings. It is from these sacred realms that I work today.

By age twenty-three, I had used up my lifetime ration of alcohol and drugs. Soon after admitting this to myelf, I met a woman named Jeanne Theodore, who became my mentor in many spheres of life. She and her husband Nick opened their home and their hearts to me. It is because of Jeanne that I am alive today. Although it has been a long time since I have needed to camp out on her den floor while going through one life crisis or another, I still call her when the going gets too rough.

I have been living the life of an artist now for over twenty-five years. In addition to tracking my dreams on canvas, I teach, though I do not teach for the masses. I have been writing as well. My first book, *Warrior Woman: A Journal of My Life As an Artist,* was composed over a five-year period and published a few weeks after my mother died. *Coyote Woman: A Continuing Journal of My Life As an Artist* picks up where that one left off—in February 1991, toward the end of our sojourn in Kingman.

These days, as I watch five-year-old Alexandra "write" in pictures, I am reminded of the power of images and words to give birth to ever deeper truths, like waves rolling one over another, farther and farther up the beach. For me, the original impetus for an intense creative drive was emotional pain; making art was a matter of life and death, of becoming mired in emotional illness or taking the difficult journey to wholeness. Today, more than nineteen years later, I can tell you that it has been an ongoing journey of recovery and growth. I believe in God, Goddess, spirits, and magic. I am filled with visions about the direction the next phase of my life will take. I am thrilled to be home in New Mexico.

Chapter 1

Shooting the Rapids

The first time I saw Coyote Woman, she was performing a sideways cat dance in the shadows that fall between consciousness and the temples of the inner world. Uninvited, she came to my rescue after a visit to the site of Fort Camp Beale, here in Kingman. The former fort is a dark place where in the late 1800s, the "good guys" interned the desert Indian tribes known collectively as the Pai, whom they had rounded up from various parts of the Mojave Desert and Colorado River areas. In this unhappy place their freedom and ways of life were taken from them, their bodies and spirits broken, and their sacred practices abruptly terminated . . .

Kingman, Arizona
February 13, 1991

After several forays my husband Bob and I were at last able to locate the site of Fort Camp Beale, which is now flattened. The residents of Kingman do not want people poking around out there; it's a historical site, they say. Actually, it has no historical signs, though it is a *spiritually* marked area, easy to find by following your heart to a wellspring of tears. The place bears the distinct imprint of human cruelty and suffering—nothing to be proud of. It's a depressing spot reeking of human defeat and surrounded by shredded barbed wire, No Trespassing signs, and a bad feeling. It has the look of a throwaway zone where local kids might go to smoke dope, although I wouldn't recommend it!

For hours after our trip to this agitated Land of the Dead, I was trailed by unhappy spirits. As twilight descended around our house, their threats became more tangible. Sensing the anger they carried like burning firebrands, I knew I was not safe, and I called my spirit allies to me. Suddenly, I was distracted by a ghostlike entity. It was a woman—or was it? She had a transparent human body and wore the skin of a coyote across her back, its head fitting over her own and its muzzle shading her face. Brandishing a wooden staff over her head, she danced sideways in and out of the purple evening shadows, shouting, "Hey, hey, hey."

The shadows fled before her as she circled and stomped. "Follow my steps," she told me. "Put your feet where mine have touched." In this way I learned the coyote dance. And ever since, nothing has moved in a straight line. My life, however, is moving forward like an avalanche down a mountain, for Coyote Woman seems to have danced me right out of Kingman. I know my work here is done.

Indian Wells, Arizona
February 16, 1991

It's flu season, and everyone else in the family has been ill. This morning Bob suggested that I get out of the house for a few days—not only to avoid coming down with the "bug" but also to placate the warring forces that at times rise up in me, fueling a rebellion that destroys the life I have built. "Just run away," he told me. So I ran hundreds of miles away to visit my longtime friend and mentor Jeanne, whom I had met on the path to recovery from alcohol and drug abuse when I was twenty-three years old and nearly dead.

As soon as I pulled out of our driveway, I seethed with anger over the loss of my life in Santa Fe and the freedom I knew before Bob and I took on the job of caring for my ailing mother. Although I reminded myself that these were changes I wanted to make, I resented that my own life had been derailed. I am physically and emotionally depleted, I mused. My mother is in and out of the hospital once or twice a month. The house is a mountain of pill bottles. Deciphering her medication schedule is a nightmare, yet one in which I must figure prominently since she can no longer keep track of what she has taken.

Turning onto the highway, I came face-to-face with a rush of fears. I feared for my sanity and physical health. I worried that my precious three year old had been robbed of her mother. The free spirit I once was, I told myself, has become buried under at-home care instructions, lengthy lists of medications, and guilt that whatever I do is nowhere near enough. Caring for an aging and sometimes loopy mother, a loving husband, and a toddler who won't let me kiss her is overwhelming. I wondered if my marriage could stand up to the strain.

Finally, I arrived at Jeanne's house. We stayed up late into the night talking, laughing, and crying. Together, we emptied the bucket of feelings I had been carrying around. In Jeanne's great canopied bed I told her of my big fears and little worries, of how hard it sometimes is to act like a grown-up. She told me it was essential to get away from my routine from time to time, maybe every three or four months. We talked of God and prayed together quietly. The relief that washed over me was medicine for my heart and spirit. I felt the gift of being known down to my soul by another human being.

Kingman, Arizona
February 17, 1991

Waking up in Jeanne's house reminded me that for the first time in four years I had spent the night away from my family. I recalled how liberating the simple act of walking out the door had felt. Before small jaunts, I was accustomed to covering every base so that no one would notice my absence or be at all inconvenienced by it. But this trip was different: I left the whole seething mass for the rest of the brood to take care of.

While driving home across desolate desert country, I had six hours to reflect on the past two years as well as the current state of my life. It's been extraordinarily lonely living in Kingman, I told myself, since the sudden death of my dad. When I received the distress call reporting his strange behavior, there was no mistaking the panic in my mother's voice. Then my father grabbed the phone and, between incoherent statements, ranted, "I'm dying, Tina!" In terror I packed Sasha into the van and tore off across the desert. Bob followed the next day.

Three days later my father was a vegetable. Two weeks after that he was dead. Unable to leave my mother alone, I had visions of driving back and forth across the desert from Santa Fe to the West Coast with a young baby in tow, to move Mom in and out of hospitals, fix disasters, and try to ease her intense grief over the loss of the man she had loved for over fifty years. That scheme was impractical, so we asked Mom to join us in the mountains of New Mexico—a move that was impossible because of her severe emphysema and accompanying heart problems. Consequently, we decided to sell her home in Nipomo, California, as well as our own in Santa Fe. Bob and I completed both transactions over the phone, never seeing our little hundred-year-old adobe again. As if that were not painful enough, the vibrant couple who had inhabited it after romancing each other across the deserts of the Southwest seemed to have disappeared from the face of the earth.

Stepping hard on the gas pedal, I recalled our confusion and desperation as we settled on moving our family of three-plus-Mom to Kingman, Arizona. It was in the desert and offered plenty of beautiful wild landscape to paint. Certainly, I admitted to myself, the mesas and mountains *are* starkly beautiful and charged with energy. I paint and write day and night. I walk the mesas, stepping through sagebrush and rarely encountering a soul. But I am lonely.

My thoughts rolled on like the narrow strip of road. Our greatest challenge in Kingman has been the dearth of community. Immersed in one of the most difficult transitions of our lives, we lack the assistance we need. There are no caregiver support groups for me to recharge in; my husband is a shadow of the man I married; and medical care for my mom is marginal. What's more, on the streets of Kingman we no doubt look as if we have been dropped from spaceships. Although the natural beauty of the place is astounding, we need people. Yes, I told myself, the decision Bob and I made the day after our visit to the site of Fort Camp Beale seems right: we must move to Tucson.

While driving on through the vast emptiness, I envisioned a painting of Coyote Woman. I saw her in her coyote headdress, dancing. As eager as I was to begin the painting, I reminded myself that changing our residence would disrupt my creative routine and that it was best to wait until our arrival in Tucson, where I'd be able to get down on the floor and stretch a four-by-six-foot canvas for her.

Oh, she's with me now. I'm about to go to sleep and I see her out of the corner of my eye.

Tucson, Arizona
March 8, 1991

I am sitting in a little office next to my mother's bedroom in a rambling desert hacienda. I loved this house the moment I saw it—from its central courtyard and its walls constructed of burnt adobe bricks to the roof-high Indian figs and cactus of every description surrounding it. My studio is unpacked and I am ready to work.

Heidi, the agent who found us this house, interests me. She would make a great woman friend, for I find myself talking to her about the most personal details of my life. Perhaps God has placed her on my path as a gift after a siege of great loneliness.

While straightening my books on a shelf this morning, I heard a barely audible voice emerge from a fetish I'd made of cholla wood and feathers that "found me" in the desert. The little figure jumped down and asked me to release him. He said that he did not want to take any of the beautiful beads and bits of bone I had given him—only a few grayish feathers and some birdseed. Of course, I did exactly as he wished; last I saw him, he was leaning against a saguaro north of here. His desire to leave marked the end of a cycle in my life, and now I am wondering if another fetish will come to take his place.

March 9, 1991

When people in Tucson ask where I am from, I tell them Santa Fe, convinced that Kingman was simply a way station on this journey I am on. Our move to Kingman is one I often play with in my mind, turning it this way and that. In addition to not knowing where else to take my mother, I had felt a gnawing need for an inward retreat. Indeed, I painted extraordinary images there, all the while dreaming myself through the crack in this world and out into other planes. I also completed my first book manuscript there.

For my inner life and creativity, Kingman was a pressure cooker, a power spot. Free of distractions, I felt as though I had leaped into a creative cauldron. After a while, however, something inside me began champing at the bit, straining to get out. By the end of our two-plus years there, I had become a herd of wild horses striving, with manes flying, to flee the moody Mojave Desert.

I am glad to be in Tucson now, where it is easy to fulfill our complex needs that went unsatisfied in Kingman. I will not be lonely here, though I might miss my aloneness.

March 19, 1991

Yesterday at a meeting, I was accosted by several people who knew me from published articles about my forthcoming book, *Warrior Woman*. What a bizarre experience *that* was. Instead of participating openly in the meeting, as planned, I began retreating into suspicious watchfulness, for I did not feel the safe anonymity I am accustomed to.

On the way home, I thought about my silence and about my initial impulse to write such a self-disclosing book. In the shadows I saw the flashing tail of Coyote Woman, and I heard her say, with laughter in her voice: "Tell them loudly, 'Here I am. Here is everything about me.' While they are looking at what you appear to be, you will be over in the sagebrush putting on another costume. Make your safe haven in the other world."

The world to which she was referring, I knew, had no parking meters, no lights, and only one big sign: Pavement Ends. That conclusion was based on an experience I had several days before while, finding my way around this spread-out desert town, I was startled by a strange configuration of flashing traffic lights. It was supposed to be a warning signal, but looked more like a beacon sending messages to spaceships. As I drove toward the little energy vortex of flip-flopping lights, something seemed to snap in the back of my neck, and I dropped through one of those psychic "gateways" that seem to open unexpectedly in response to visual stimuli, music, trance states, or dancing. Immediately in front of me I saw, with crystal clarity, a slit in the fabric of everyday life, and a moment later I was surrounded by laughing horses. I then heard the disembodied sound of my *own* laughter.

Wispy veils hung at my side. As I brushed against transparent walls, I knew in my solar plexus that my being was changing. It is vital to ignore the definitions and expectations others have of me, a voice was saying, because those identities and roles have become shackles. To grow through this cycle of change, I must divest myself of all mooring lines.

I popped out at the red light at Dodge and River Streets, and drove on home. It was another ordinary nonordinary day.

I am still cooking the Coyote Woman painting on low heat and am not yet ready to let her loose in the house. In the meantime, to enlarge my painting space, I'm having a long wall in the living room taken down. I believe in using the "living" room for painting, rather than treating it like a mausoleum, and have hired Garth, a local contractor, to do the work. We'll be adding two sets of French doors to the room, as well as overhead fans. Garth knows I want to turn this living room into my studio as soon as possible so that I can take my supplies out of storage and begin to stretch a big canvas.

There is something exhilarating about working under adverse conditions. Perhaps it is the confidence that comes from knowing in your gut that nothing is going to stop you from doing what you need to do. Without my electric staple gun, however, I quake in canvasophobia.

On Sunday, Bob and I went Saint Francis Church, across the arroyo from our home, for what turned out to be a rowdy celebration attended by interesting people—weird, even. We fit right in! I'm planning to see about renting a room there for an Artists' Recovery Through the Steps (ARTS) meeting. ARTS is a 12-step program designed to help people find and activate their creative centers. I, for one, need this type of spiritual focus on my art right now.

March 22, 1991

The moon is waxing and I'm wired to the hilt, which has left me strung out and smiling insanely—wound up just a little too tight. Certain that I can complete everything on my myriad lists, I am here at the computer while the rest of the household sleeps.

Ideas for new paintings are flying into my mind like a runaway slide show. My only hope for keeping up with these images is to cover the desk, the walls, even the dashboard of my car with Post-it note sketches of them all. Every scrap of paper in my pockets and purses is already covered with beautiful sketches.

My greatest efforts, however, are focused on writing. The thrust to put my finishing touches on the book has my brain on red alert, saying, "Finish it—hurry. Be done with it." *Warrior Woman* is crowning and I'm bearing down hard, pushing her out into the world with all my might. At the same time, I can hardly imagine what a published book will mean to this terminally shy person.

My husband has a book out that contains stories of our lives. At a recent social gathering, a woman told me she had read about me in both his book and a variety of recent articles. She said she now knows all about me and yet I know nothing about her and isn't that ironic and weird and neat. It so happens that I *did* know something about her: her name was Janee and, according to a comment she had made earlier, she liked to create things using her hands. Although I appreciated what she had to say at the beginning of the get-together, during our encounter I felt like a deer caught in the headlights of an oncoming bus. Later, I saw my discomfort as a reaction posed by adjusting to an unfamiliar place and getting to know new people.

How strange it is to lead a public life! Yet this is only the beginning of it all, for soon my personal journal will be seeing the light of day. As scared as I am about putting *Warrior Woman* out into the world, I am determined to see it through, since I have been striving for recognition as an artist and writer these last twenty years. I will do whatever it takes to be at peace with her emergence.

Lately, I have been projecting many of my self-doubts and feelings of disapproval onto my mother, who is living out her dying with us. Whenever I think of her picking up my book, I experience an irrepressible urge to censor everything I have written. Curiously, as of now she has no idea that I've written anything other than a few articles. I cannot figure out whether by not telling her about my book I'm acting like an adolescent trying to get away with something, an adult liberated from having to check everything out with mommy, or simply a person in need of a life far beyond the intrusive reach of the beloved familial octopus. No doubt, all of these motives, and more, are true.

While visiting a showroom-warehouse in a downtown industrial district yesterday, I bought some Mexican furniture and asked the owner to please deliver it. When he arrived, he saw my paintings, fell in love with them, and asked to exhibit them in his shop. The setting is just strange enough to be appealing, and the exhibit a welcome opportunity to get some press, to let people know I'm here in Tucson painting up a storm.

Making the art business work after moving to a new town takes considerable research. Ultimately, I would like to turn the house into a studio-gallery, but first I'll need to test the waters by talking to local folks who have been here a while. One center of operations would certainly make financial sense for now, since I do not yet have a steady enough income to pay outside rent on a regular basis. I would also like four fascinating students. Toward that end, I have left business cards at the massage center I go to, which seems to attract interesting people. Word of mouth, I have found, is often the best method for finding students.

The mind of an artist moves in creative directions to come up with ways to produce income, and mine is no exception. After all, my art must support itself, and then some. Supporting such an expensive habit is no easy feat, considering the supplies that must be purchased. A five-by-six-foot canvas that I stretch myself costs between fifty and one hundred dollars. Good oil paints, brushes, and painting medium are costly as well. One of my favorite teachers, Arnold Schifrin, taught me to buy the very best I can afford, and so I do, since purchasing art supplies amounts to investing in my emotional and spiritual well-being.

April 9, 1991

I am experiencing great resistance to hanging my paintings at the showroom downtown. I don't want to arrange for it; I don't want to go there. This impregnable part of me is like a three-year-old child. The best approach for now is to call the showroom people and apologize for my delay. I'll feel better having at least reestablished communication with them.

April 14, 1991

The moon is peeking at me through the mesquite tree that fans gracefully outside my office window. I am feverishly revising portions of *Warrior Woman* so that she can go to the editor. This is the most tedious experience I have ever had. I may never write again.

April 29, 1991

We have just returned from an extraordinary trip to the Yucatán, where Bob and I put on our first workshop together. We spent an entire week introducing participants to the channels we use for opening ourselves emotionally and creatively. I had brought along a number of carefully chosen cassettes to furnish background music. In addition, each participant had oil pastels and a big sketchbook for experimentation in self-expression, as well as a journal and pen for recording stream-of-consciousness responses.

We drew, wrote, wept, and laughed till our sides split open and our guts spilled out onto the pink marble floor. We danced in the entrails as they lay there red and pulsating. The locals who saw or heard us asked repeatedly what we were doing in that room: "*¿Qué hacen?*" "*¿Quién sabe?*"

Each one of us stretched in one way or another. Conducting a week-long workshop, I have found, is ideal. No matter what, there is growth—even in participants who initially appear "stuck."

When the workshop ended, Bob and I took off for an underground river in the town of Scaret, in Quintana Roo. As soon as I saw the steps leading to the rocks below, I had no choice but to descend into the earth to swim in this pale phosphorescent blue. At first touch, the warm water brought great physical pleasure. Then the more I swam, the more I lost track of time and space until I felt as if I had merged with The Woman Who Is the River, La Femme Qui Est La Rivière—a figure I painted many years back, before the river of life came and took me.

Bob and I also visited Chichén Itzá, the best known of all Maya ruins, where we climbed inside the Temple of the Warriors. After entering the pyramid through a narrow passageway seemingly robbed of oxygen, we clambered up sixty steps on feet, knees, and hands, like little snarling jungle cats. At the top was a chamber graced by the reclining figure of Chac-mool, who in central Mexico is associated with human sacrifice. His smile conveyed an unmistakable message: "I am the last thing you will see in this lifetime." His companion in the swelteringly small chamber was a small red stone jaguar sweetly baring two rows of perfect little white teeth. Her compact body was inlaid with disks of green jade, and her eyes were hypnotic green. Such gracious and voracious hosts! An ancient fear vibrated throughout the chamber which, we were not surprised to learn, most people only visit once.

April 30, 1991

I started the morning with a cold swim, after which Bob and I went to a yoga class. Heidi's daughter Meigen, a gifted young artist, came to paint in the afternoon. Together, we christened the studio. She painted a red "spirit horse" flying out of the clouds while I worked on a skull. Although I could not find my palette (the current "dis-routine" is more stimulating than order and predictability, even if everything does take twice as long this way), I reveled in the beautiful and open workspace. The French doors and overhead fans brought in plenty of air and light. My mother even wandered through a few times like a wraith, her moccasins scuffing along the floor. I was glad to see her upright, and she was happy to see me painting.

As soon as Meigen's lesson ended, I hurried off to a local stable and jumped on a horse—inspired, perhaps, by her painting. I spent a magnificent hour and a half riding up into the Santa Catalina Mountains, all the while admiring the cactus flowers. The prickly pear were exploding with yellow and cognac-colored blossoms, reminding me of how intensely emotional and heartbreakingly brief the desert blooming season is.

This evening I soaked in an Epsom salt–sesame oil–seaweed bath to ease out my knees, still sore from the ride. Now I am looking back on a day filled with everything that makes me happy to be alive. My life has been rendered in the most vivid colors.

May 3, 1991

It's 4:00 A.M. Two hours ago I was awakened from a sound sleep by an ominous thump followed by wailing, both emanating from Sasha's room. Dashing in to see what had happened, I found that she had flown out of the upper trundle on her "big-girl bed" and landed with a thud. Finding her on the carpet, I comforted her and tucked her in the lower bed. Although I've been dumping in all manner of herbal teas for an hour, I'm unable to relax enough to go back to sleep.

The wretched skull painting irritates me every time I look at it. I hate the cursed thing. The white skull on the canvas painted turquoise has no strength to it, no life in it. Evidently, new forces are pushing my paintings, but the direction they are moving in has not yet become clear.

Last night I was working on a painting of a cross—one of my favorite designs. To me, the cross suggests something distinctly pagan, a meeting place for spirits where anything can happen. Initially, my desire to paint crosses shocked me; after all, I'd spent nine unpleasant years as a non-Catholic child in a Catholic school where the liturgy and symbols seemed inapplicable to the unbaptized. The implication was that we non-Catholic children would sooner or later be burning in hell. Ancient wisdom, however, infused the crosses with a more universal meaning and gave them back to me. In my dreams women wrapped in blankets began telling me it was right to paint my crosses with lightning bolts and snakes. Now my walls are filled with these symbols of wholeness and healing.

Beyond my walls are more signs of nature. At the moment, a mourning dove is singing sadly outside my window, sending forth an emotionally evocative sound. Throwing the window open to listen, I am transported back to the airy room I grew up in. The big tree outside my childhood window offered sanctuary to a variety of birds both day and night. On otherwise quiet afternoons my bedroom would fill with blue and purple shadows and birdsong.

Here in our Tucson "game refuge," each morning brings a winged parade. We are visited by cactus wrens, woodpeckers, and other desert birds that make soft nests in the woody pockets inside the saguaros growing on our land. At first, they poke in and out of their formidable little houses. Then, come sunrise, we are treated to a concert of pecking—on our house, the metal swamp coolers, the mesquite trees that surround us—raising a ruckus that drives Bob crazy. I have made him promise not to go out and shoot at the insolent little red-bereted buggers. But despite his promise, they seem to know how much he hates them, for when he steps outside they do everything but give him the finger.

Playa Blanca, Mexico
May 15, 1991

This evening after dinner at our hotel, as Sasha and I walked beneath the branches of flower-laden trees, my gaze was drawn steadily toward the swimming pool, which glowed with an intense blue light. We approached the water's edge, sat on some nearby steps, and mesmerized by the tropical air, stared into the luminous water. Immediately, the blue of the water triggered the memory of a dream I had twenty years ago, when I first began tracking my dreams and painting them. As vividly as in the dream, I saw a pale woman sitting on the same step I was on and looking through the water into an opening that was lit from the depths by an intense blue light.

The dream, although I knew it held great meaning, had an ominous feel to it that frightened me. Each time I recalled the image, I became so terrified that the hair on the back of my neck shot up and I felt myself pulling away. These were no doubt healthy responses of a young woman who, peering over the rim into a vortex, wanted to melt into the blueness, but not knowing what she would find there, was wary of being seduced into the dreamworld. Later, I drew an image of the dream woman looking into the indigo and washed by the pervasive blue light that shone upward from its mysterious source. As it has turned out, the woman on the edge of the abyss, pondering the blue light radiating from the earth, foretold of my descent into the interior and the ensuing emergence of my own strength!

Over the years, this imagery remained alive as a vivid memory. Here and there, I would stumble upon elements of the dream out in the so-called real world. While in a dinghy in Capri, a thrill coursed through me as I opened my unsuspecting eyes in the underground caverns of the

Blue Grotto and recognized the unmistakable hue; I threw off my dress and plunged into the pool that glowed in the darkness. In Brazilia, I wandered into a church constructed solely of blue glass, its interior saturated with blue light. I was washed away in blue.

Through painting, ritual work, visions, and dream tracking, I soon became acquainted with the unexplored caves, bottomless lakes, and underground rivers of my being. Barefoot, I began treading through every jungle, city, mountain, sea, desert, and river of myself. Many times I walked these paths in darkness, only to discover that they were ancient trails well-worn by other women's feet and traceable—through our pain, tears, and knowings—all the way back to First Woman.

Here in Playa Blanca, as I sat in the same position on the same step that appeared in my dream of long ago, I was struck by the sense that once again something extraordinary was about to unfold in my life. I had returned to one of the initiatory visions that first led me to my path—only now I was with my daughter and we were *two* radiant beings looking into the great feminine source. Side by side, washed in blue, we sat sharing the darkness and the light, gazing dreamily into the deep pool of indigo.

Tucson, Arizona
May 19, 1991

We returned last night from our idyllic trip to Playa Blanca. The ocean was warm, clear, and waveless—the way I like it. While snorkling for the first time, I entered the undulating world of coral castles. I gasped through my snorkel at the startling colors of the fish while making fish dances with my hands in greeting. They played back and often came swimming across my mask.

The return trip was interminable, however, and we arrived home from the magnificent week in wretched condition. When one travels, the gods are either with you or against you. You make all your connections or none. You can sleep in an airport for days, never seeing a loved one or finding your tweezers. My approach to air travel is to enter into an altered state and doggedly do whatever is required to get home.

The most troubling part of this return trip was flying over Joshua

Tree, California, where I was flooded with sadness. Like the beat of a drum you can't quite ignore, I sensed that another wave of change was coming, that the tide was about to go out, taking pieces of my life away with it. Not knowing what is coming is so frightening it makes me want to run, and yet messages of this sort remind me to await the hand of God. One thing is certain: I have been alerted of an impending shift.

Among the most promising aspects of the return flight were thoughts of painting. Although I took art supplies with me to Playa Blanca, I never touched them. (I seldom feel the desire to paint while on the road.) Partway home, however, the yearning to make art came down upon me with urgency. Once back in the studio, I looked at the giant painting of the skull and decided that it was pretty wonderful after all. The turquoise field, after many hours of struggle, appeared more intense, and the whites more agitated. It's good to see something alive on the easel.

I also began incubating a painting of Mexico's representation of the Black Madonna—the Virgin of Guadalupe. I have several images of her in my writing room and more in my bedroom. I'm listening for her to tell me how she wants to be painted. The Virgin of Guadalupe loves to talk to artists!

May 23, 1991

This morning, as I approached the easel and picked up my brush, I concluded that the glorious skull painting looked like shit! Giving it more layers of paint, I noticed the turquoise richening up. Then as I brought in some blue-tinged mineral violet from the edges, blending and melting, the painting began to deepen. It is a mysterious icon now—a symbol of the Southwest desert, that which is larger and more enduring than life yet at the same time apt to crumble with the passage of time. The painting is big and now truly beautiful; I get a wiggly feeling in my solar plexus while looking at it.

Next I worked on what has evolved into a series of cross paintings. Why, I wonder, is this image so loaded for me? And why have I filled my house with it? The cross, I decided, is a little square mandala, a visual symbol of something profound that has taken place within me after so many years of therapy and self-examination. It reveals a linking up of disparate elements, a weaving together of the pieces of the self that I have painstakingly gathered after wandering through the galaxy, especially the Place of Bones, looking for my lost, broken, and amputated parts. Connections are taking place in the deepest layer of my being. The cross, then, serves as both a postcard portraying where I have been and a map showing me the way home.

After more than twenty years of therapy, my body is united with my feelings; my feelings are united with my mind; and my mind is hitched to my spirit. As a result, my intuitive faculties are fully operational and chattering, whether or not I want to hear from them. I have spent decades holding court from my throne in gutters and underground rivers, all the while meeting and conversing with the strange cast of characters that populate my unconscious. And now the balanced, self-contained little crosses celebrate the integration that has permitted connections to take place without my conscious participation. I am healthy and whole, even when the proverbial shit connects with the Big Fan.

Chapter 2

A Woman Flying over the Desert

Tucson, Arizona
June 1, 1991

I am unable to contact my inner guides and spirits. They must have left for a while, as they sometimes do, forcing me to increase my participation in the outer world. Without communication from the other side, I feel lonely and merely three-dimensional. My night dreams are busy but flat; my daydreams, active yet frustrating. I am missing real communication with myself.

June 4, 1991

It is done—hot damn! This noontime I took the whole writhing mass of *Warrior Woman*—including the slides, shards, matchbook covers, and bits of sparkly confetti—and crammed it into a Federal Express envelope to fly on eagles' wings to the printer. After all these months of back and forth, send this and we need that, I was higher than a kite approaching the Milky Way. Deep in the unnavigable jungle, tribal peoples dropped their weapons and gave a shout of elation that shook me. Drums beat in intricate rhythms; feet stamped in unison. Celebration lit up the darkest, farthest corners of the kingdom. Electrical circuits that had been shut down came back on, and I returned to the living.

Finishing the book was an accomplishment involving all the gods and goddesses of the past, present, and future. Amazed and filled with gratitude, I am no longer fearful of being sucked into the Land Where Writers Never Write Again.

June 6, 1991

Today the family dog Bella, a silky brown Doberman, got into a jam I could not get her out of. She dashed in front of a car and was run over. We heard her howling in pain on the road. It turned out that her pelvis was crushed, broken in three places. We put her down.

When it was over, Bob and I went out to Sabino Canyon—a good place to go when there's crying to be done. There I saw her gentle face and loving eyes in the flying white thunderheads above us. Images of her racing with me through the magical mesas in Kingman showed her happy and free as a much loved dog can be. Her spirit stayed close to us all afternoon.

As we left Sabino, I felt sick at the thought of never stroking her satin head again. Turning on some classical music, I drove toward the flaming setting sun. Red rain was falling in a circle around us as I called out silently, "I won't forget you, silky ears."

June 8, 1991

Last night when I turned off the light, I could have sworn I felt a dog jump on the bed. Once I got over my fright, I mentally gathered up the space where a dog used to be.

Our house is a sadder place without Bella's exuberant spirit. It is especially empty at my writing desk, where she was always in my way, her long legs tangled around the legs of my chair. I want her to bother me, to bump up against my elbow as my fingers fly across the keyboard.

I have been crying nearly nonstop since we lost Bella, and now I see there is a much bigger river of sadness welling up *behind* my grief for her. I cannot decipher which tears belong to which loss; I am just letting them pour out. It's the sort of experience you want to go through with your dog by your side, which right now is precisely what is happening: I am in a black and silver gondola gliding through the Land of the Dead. Bella is with me. I feel her love and protection all around me.

I remember the day I sent off my manuscript and proceeded to spend nearly half an hour stroking Bella's beautiful head and ears, looking into her soft brown eyes, and telling her she was my "doggie girl." She, in turn, was drunk with joy. Her head was lolling, her eyes were closing—she was nearly fainting with love. I am glad we had that time together before she was suddenly gone. As for me, I have lost a true friend. Someone who loved me completely is gone forever.

June 12, 1991

I've just finished painting the fourth *cruz*. This one has two Mojave green rattlers forming a cross within the main adobe-colored cross—a color combination that is new for me. A deep ordering of my self is taking place as I dive into each of these little mandalas. Meanwhile, the house is filling with them. These enigmatic twelve-by-fourteen-inch pieces look just as strong as the five-by-twelve-foot painting hanging next to them.

Earlier in the day, having come across a slide of an oil pastel piece I did in the Yucatán, I bought a canvas so I could paint it in a larger format. My artwork is shifting planes again. Pictures float upward like photographic impressions rising to the surface in the darkroom. Unfamiliar imagery flickers by as I stare off into space. The crosses punctuate these new visions.

Looking out my window, I see that the desert needs a thunderstorm. The sky has a thick cover of clouds. The mesquites are motionless; the birds still, for once. From time to time, the unnerving electric song of a cicada cracks the silence. I'm going to get out my oil pastel piece, prop it up, and look at it for a while before putting it to canvas. I am hoping for a downpour; I need some rain.

June 13, 1991

The rains have come! Amid deafening thunder, the water is washing away not only tension that has built up throughout the city but also the griminess of our lives—our crimes and misdemeanors.

Tears well up in pools of relief. Lovers take to their beds. We are one with the Mother, one with the sky and the earth. We are her children dancing with joy at the beauty of her blessing. Rain in the desert is a great deal more than "precipitation."

Two students are coming today, and I plan to accomplish a lot of painting while they are here. On the easel is the piece I've started from the Yucatán sketch: a woman flying through the sky with two snakes, a radiant daughter of the sun. The snakes are her protectors and guides. One—a winged, coiled creature—symbolizes the gathering of power.

June 17, 1991

Two nights ago Bob, Sasha, and I went out for a twilight hike. Because we're in the midst of high rattlesnake season, I took along a flashlight. At first, nothing crossed our paths except for a *cucaracha* that took a liking to us and followed us for a short distance like a stray dog. As we walked up our driveway, however, I noticed a sinuous ripple of light in the sand. Flipping on the flashlight, I saw a small red-and-yellow-banded king snake.

This jeweled beauty seemed frightened by our looming presence, but soon calmed down. Sasha, unafraid, stood transfixed. I gently touched the creature's glistening skin and watched as it tried to enter small holes in the earth, winding its way down, then corkscrewing back out.

Yesterday I attended a service at Saint Francis Church, across the arroyo from us. The service was emotionally engaging, as was the abundance of music and controversy. I came away feeling touched by the hand of God. I consider myself an automatic member of open-minded churches such as this one, a freelance member of the greater laughing, breathing, heaving spiritual body.

The churches I am attracted to are teeming with action, dissension, and love. They give without excluding, judging, banning, forbidding, or condemning. Their denomination does not matter; nor do I care what name their ministers use when referring to God, or whether they speak of "he," "she," or "it." To me, God is God. I need the spiritual stimulation offered by such churches, yet I abhor dogma. I won't tolerate control from a church. I won't subject my child to the sneaky conversion, subversion, and perversion of the self—manipulations that in traditional and Fundamentalist churches tend to focus strongly on women. And I don't like the word *sin*—too many years of Catholic school, I suppose. Oh, I definitely believe in right and wrong; I simply don't like the S word.

Of course, one need not go to church to get hooked up to the source. Often it is better to go out for a hike and let God find you in the desert, or to listen to the cactus wrens and the mourning doves. Still, it is a profound experience to sit in a roomful of people reaching toward God.

So there I was yesterday, Father's Day, with tears streaming down my face during most of the service. My father is not in this world anymore; my sister is dead; my mother is leaving, slowly and painfully. The losses I am facing fill me with fear and sadness, for there is no retrieving the ones we love from the Land of the Dead. My beloved mother, although she is not yet there, is not really here either. No longer do I feel that I am walking alongside her. I don't know how to make contact with her, and I am not sure how much contact I want to make. I'm afraid that if we maintain our closeness, something inside me will decide to leave with her.

I am experiencing primitive terror at the thought of living in the world without this old soul who loves me so deeply. When she is gone, who will know me in the way she does? Who will protect me in the dark and scary night? What will I be when she leaves? Lonely . . . and alone. An orphan in this world.

A strange dance is going on tonight between the moon, Jupiter, Venus, and Mars. I think it is affecting my work and my dreams, all of which seem charged with electricity.

June 21, 1991

It is summer solstice, a day marking the balance of light and darkness. In honor of the occasion I went into the desert this evening to dance, and after only a few steps, out came Coyote Woman. I could feel her pointy, cunning nose pushing through to my face, and her tufted gray ears springing up on my head.

With her tail switching seductively, Coyote Woman pranced and trotted, on guard, ears pricked. Lifting her damp black nose, she read the winds while circling the dancing grounds again and again. When she finished, I dropped to the earth, panting and sweating. In my collapsed state I thought about painting her. Painting her, I reasoned, would be relatively easy after *being* her.

At the end of the solstice ceremony, I slithered into the warm Sonoran night and walked until I came to our pool. There I shrugged off my black dancing skirt and top, slipped out of my sneakers, and jumped into the moon-filled water. While submerged in the water, which was both cooling and warm, I washed off the residue of ritual.

Water in the desert is magnetic, and wind is a sorceress. Floating there amid the *clack-clack* of the palm fronds blowing in the breeze, I gave myself over to the desert forces. Before stepping back into my sneakers, I shook each one out to dislodge all visitors; I had no desire to meet a scorpion in my shoe! Then slowly I strode to my moonlit bedroom, wrapped myself in cool white sheets, and fell into a dreamless sleep. I'd already done my dreaming for the night.

June 29, 1991

I am struggling with the painting of the woman flying over the desert. There is something new in it that I can't quite grasp. Although I resist working on this outstretched figure of the sky goddess with the sun radiating from behind her, she fascinates me. I'm going to work on this piece till I get it right.

One day last week we went to the circus with Sasha. When I was young, I didn't like the circus and saw nothing funny about the clowns. As an adult, I attend the circus whenever it comes to town. I get seats in one of the first few rows so I can see everything, then once the show begins, I laugh till I think I might explode. Going with Sasha was glorious. I found myself looking at her as much as at the performers. Flickering across her angelic face was astonished pleasure mixed with innocence, wonder, and pure delight.

During the performance, Sasha asked repeatedly for a red toy sword.

When it comes to toys, our policy is to look over all available items and pick the "best one"—which is what she did, never wavering from the sword. After the elephants and tigers departed, we trooped up to the concession stand, where she asked for a red sword that blinked off and on. She didn't want the small sparkly variety; she wanted the "big one."

Wordlessly intent when we returned home, Sasha stepped away from the car and the circle of house lights, walked into the darkness, and brandishing her blinking sword, called aloud, "Come here, all you monsters!" How glad I was that we had let her choose her weapon; at the age of three, she knew what was needed to get the job done. The raw material is there in *all* of us at the beginning.

I brought home two solid black kittens from the pound several weeks ago. They are male and female littermates, and we named them both Puma. It is important to implant illogical wisdom in my child early on; this way, I'm less likely to end up with a prissy twelve year old telling me in a voice dripping with disgust, "M-o-o-o-m, you can't give *both* cats the *same name*." For now, the advantage is that we don't have to stop and figure out which cat is which; it is always Puma.

There are now two small black clowns whirling through my office, my desk, and my life. Several days ago they climbed onto Bob's desk when he was out of the room. While playing on the keyboard, they changed the name of his manuscript to "666777**pooolI." I wonder what other literary assistance they have provided.

July 3, 1991

I slipped my moorings and sailed into another realm with the help of a little music and a somewhat unorthodox therapist–travel guide named Lynn Namka. There I met a dancing woman. I heard her before I saw her, and what I heard were bells—*chink-achink-achink*. Wearing a tunic of midnight blue, red leggings, and bands of bells on her wrists and ankles, she was dancing in the dark, her feet lightly stamping on the dusty ground.

"What are you doing here?" I asked. "I am the finest dancer of many, many tribes," she replied. "I represent the women. It is an honor to be here dancing, to be seen as the best. It is all right to step to the front of the line and lead. We all need another woman to hold a light in front of us as we go along in life." *Chink-chink-chink-chank.* Her braids danced as she stamped in a circular pattern back into the shadows.

Chapter 3

The Grandmothers Come

Tucson, Arizona
July 11, 1991

Yesterday I began, and more or less completed, a painting of Dancing Woman with bells on her wrists and ankles, and her blue-black braids flying. I then made wristbands and anklets decorated with large silver bells. Slipping them on, I stamped out several steps, listening to the *chink-chink* of the clappers and feeling the tinkling magic conveyed by their sound.

While dancing, I spotted a favorite small drum made from hollowed-out bamboo; when struck, a beautiful knocking sound reverberated from its innards. I took this drum, together with the wristbands, anklets, and the painting of Dancing Woman, to a gathering of women at Lynn Namka's house. There we made music and told tales of our lives, all the while laughing and weeping together.

Part of what I explored with the group was the anger I feel being in the same house with my mother. I described my ambivalence about telling her I have written a book. While talking, I could feel that in back of my anger was a pervasive fear still lingering from childhood, when alcoholic violence seemed perennially poised to rip my beloved mother from my life. I have always been afraid of her death; now I live with its approach on a daily basis. It breathes raspily in the darkness under her bed that sometimes smells of rotting flesh, and in her closet, where my father's ashes hover in a cardboard box and his musty, lived-in, well-made clothes hang neatly in a corner. Death permeates my mother's room, waiting for me to face it, waiting as always to take her from me before I think I can live without her.

I called out from these dark passages of my being, after which a voice from another world loudly proclaimed, "You are our daughter. You always have been and always will be. Nature, where you find such comfort and guidance, is your mother. When your earthly mother dies, you will belong to us. And when you leave the earth plane, you will hand your own daughter over to us to raise and care for." It is no wonder Namka calls our group "Women of Spirit, Women of Power."

Today, while flying inward like a bat entering a cave, I asked why I am living with my mother as she prepares to leave this life. From deep inside came an answer: "It is a payback from long, long ago." Once I have helped her exit this world that she helped me enter, I realized, everything will be done between us. Yes, there will be tears and sadness, but also completion, strength, and freedom. From the searing fires of loss I will emerge initiated into a new life.

July 25, 1991

Over these past few days I've experienced another wave of intense anger toward my mother. It's very difficult to live with your mother, no matter how wonderful she is and how much she tries to stay out of the way. It's a primal predicament—too many females in the same cave.

This afternoon I took a nap so I could dream. In the dream my mother and I were eating challah—one of the most beautiful breads in the world. When I woke up, I jumped into my car and went out looking for a loaf of this braided bread. After a few unsuccessful stops, I located a perfect loaf, brought it home, and used it to lure my mother from her bed to the kitchen table. Bread, she has often said, is her favorite food. And sure enough, to the table she came, as did Sasha, whereupon the three of us ate the challah with great pleasure. Since Mother and I broke bread together, things have been less tense between us.

The linear gauntlet of proofreading *Warrior Woman* has impacted on my painting. I could step up to the easel and slap some paint on Our

Lady of Guadalupe with her pink snakes, but to reenter the realm of the spirits, I must trick the logical brain and escape from it through a doorway glimpsed in a dream.

Several people have asked me, "Don't you pay to have someone else do the editing?" I do, but the writer still has to read every word over and over again. Writers, editors, proofreaders—we all make mistakes. The best one thus far was a typo that appeared when the cover mock-up arrived for my approval: the title read, "Worrier Woman." That was the day I began to worry in earnest.

July 27, 1991

Bob and I have just returned from a glorious weekend in Aspen. When he announced that we would all take the weekend together as one big happy family, I was fit to be tied. Noticing the flames flaring from my nostrils, he then came up with the idea of going by ourselves rather than bringing the child and turning into pack mules. So it was that we spent our days in Aspen horseback riding, hiking, gabbing with our feet up, and enjoying luscious meals.

Having been well seen to, I feel like myself again. I am reenergized, considerably less pissed, and able to remember why we got married in the first place. Married couples need several escapes a year, even if only to a local campground—anything to get away from the TV, bills, phone, and rug rats. A trip away from one's kid is the marital equivalent of at least three months of therapy!

July 31, 1991

Suddenly exhausted and defeated by too many sore throats and breathing problems, I went to see Marilyn Gilbert, a gifted body worker. As she worked on me, I floated inward and noticed that psychic debris in my inner landscape was seriously aggravating my physical health. Marilyn called my attention to cold areas dotting my body and to my back which, by contrast, was feverishly hot. I told her I wanted relief for my sore throat because I was worried about passing an infection on to my debilitated mother, who had already been hospitalized numerous times with pneumonia.

I returned home and, following Marilyn's instructions, made a special cayenne pepper tea. After finishing the tea, I submerged myself in the hot waters of my little cauldron in the desert. Before long, I had warmed my body back to life.

A few hours later I went to Namka's house for a gathering of the women's group. There I carefully smudged myself with clouds of cedar smoke and took my turn speaking as the "talking stick" made its way around the circle. After each of us had spoken of our day-to-day lives, we moved to our feet, whereupon mine automatically began an odd dance. In my hands I envisioned a wide, flat basket of corn. Feeling a strong wind blow through the house, I let it move through me, all the while exhaling every milliliter of air I was able to push out of my body. Concave and empty, I sucked in the wind, the breath of life.

Soon a winged form of Crow Woman materialized, dancing lightly in coiling and uncoiling spirals while directing thin transparent threads of light into all the vacant places inside me. Air and light flowed freely into my lungs as I, too, danced, shaking particles of death out the ends of my fingertips and off my feet like a cat stepping out of a puddle. As if from a great distance, I observed the glowing threads in my chest and watched them move down through my feet, sending roots deep into the earth.

Emerging from this vision, I knew that a major change had occurred. I had been affected on the physical as well as the spiritual plane.

August 15, 1991

My mother is in the hospital with pneumonia again, although she looks better now than she did five days ago when she was admitted. I try to stay in the moment, yet most of the time the moment is filled with pain. The tension I feel would be more bearable if I were doing serious "maintenance crying." I know there's a waterfall of tears yearning to come out, because when I'm at church, I cry through most of the celebration. I need to find a way to keep the river flowing.

Other intriguing insights have come through trancing. One evening after taking my mother to the hospital, I settled down, closed my eyes, and asked Crow Woman how to come to terms with the long trail of pain that was stretching out before me. "Can you help me accept these changes?" I asked. "Go directly into the fire," she said, pointing to a place behind me. Turning around, I faced a wall of blazing flames and saw a woman on a white horse riding deliberately into them. Hair, mane, and clothing flared and burned, then woman and horse came out the other side reduced to mere bones. The answer to my question was clear: I was to head into the pain, and on the other side of the all-consuming fire I would find peace. The pain, like the fire, was not a form of punishment, but rather a means of initiation.

I have also been working with a *curandera* named Zelima—a healing woman from the jungles of Central America—on the creation of a medicine necklace. My first instruction was to visit a little store that turned out to be as weird as the shopkeeper. Under the counter, hidden beneath mounds of rhinestones and rubber spiders, were a myriad of strange beads, including some made of bone carved in the shape of skulls and others made of carved seeds. After looking around this "voodoo priestess Wal-Mart," I picked out seven turquoise disks; small bird, fox, and horse fetishes; round beads of rose quartz, peridot, malachite, and tiger's-eye; and a few special ingredients to form into a power object that would suspend from the necklace.

It took an entire ninety-minute session to string the beads and tie the knots; the knots had to be formed in silence and with "absolute awareness." The next meeting was devoted to making the clasp, itself a thing of beauty in which each knot was tied with an intention, a prayer, and a desire woven in. When the clasp was fastened on, Zelima asked if I wanted her to read my necklace, which of course I did. Taking it in her charged hands, she spun out words, slowly feeling for information as she fingered each stone: "There is past-life stuff in here. You have been a very powerful, much loved clan mother. You helped many people. In this life you still gather groups of people to you wherever you go, for you know how to guide others from the heart. In addition, you knew about herbs and healing—knowledge that you also retain in this life. As before, you find yourself ranging outdoors in search of healing herbs."

The hair on the back of my neck stood on end as Zelima continued, "You were very beautiful and had to be extremely disciplined so that vanity would not overshadow your wisdom." She encouraged me to continue to disregard appearances both in the way I live my life and in the choices I make.

I wore my necklace home and, too exhausted to take it off, lay down on my bed and dropped instantly into a dream. Zelima the *curandera* appeared with her long, straight, dark hair and jungle-cat eyes, although in the dream she was a man. Passionately, we embraced and became lovers. My sense was that she was psychically entering me.

I woke up agitated, then undressed and settled into bed for the night, still wearing my necklace. Sometime later, the dream body of Zelima appeared at my side and guided me into a straight-backed Mexican chair. Then she stepped behind me, placed her hands on either side of my back, and gently applied pressure, whereupon my spine gave a crack and shattered. Every bone in my upper torso felt broken, and I woke up quaking. I knew I was in the hands of a powerful teacher and I was never going to be the same.

August 21, 1991

Last night I attended the women's group at Namka's house, where I wept uncontrollably. Usually, crying lets off accumulated tension, but all I felt was increased misery. Before I left, Namka asked if I would like her to do some "pullouts" on me. Although I neither knew nor cared what pullouts were, I welcomed her offer. For one thing, I was certain that any undertaking would feel better than the pain I was in. For another, Namka had recently returned from a Sun Dance in South Dakota and was fully centered, radiating an irresistible presence.

After everyone else left, she sat on one end of the couch, while I lay down with my head butting up against her crossed legs, closed my eyes, and slipped away from this world. Next thing I knew, Namka was moving her hands through the air just inches from my body, and making flicking motions. "What am I pushing away?" she asked. "Iridescent blue-green bugs—big, fat flat ones," I replied. "Scarabs."

"Who else is here?" she inquired. "I am Great-Grandmother," said a low but distinct voice, "and I am here because she called for help. We are all here—all her Mothers and Grandmothers. We come from the many clans whose blood flows through her veins."

"Are you a part of Tina or outside of her?" Namka asked. "A part of her and out front, as well as behind her," Great-Grandmother replied. "We are here to take care of her. She wants to learn and we are here to teach her. She summoned us and we have come, as we always will."

Taking the tips of Namka's fingers, Great-Grandmother placed them over my aching eyes. No tears came, although my throat began to hurt as if someone were choking me. Great-Grandmother then placed Namka's hands on my throat, which tightened even more. "Stay with the feeling," Namka whispered. I did, and within seconds, a racking wave-like movement starting in my toes had passed into my calves and up through the rest of my resistant body. Out it came, with a torrent of noise and a smashing of armor.

I have no idea how long I lay writhing on Namka's couch, growling and crying. Eventually, however, peace began to pass through me with the same wavelike motion as before, at which point Namka rested her hands a few inches from my face. Looking skyward with my eyes still closed, I saw her as a raven woman scanning the mesas and arroyos. With her earthly hands she began a sweeping motion, and as I heard her working her healing in both worlds—*Scat! Scat! Scat!*—relief flooded over me. "What am I sweeping away?" she asked. A voice deeper than my own replied from within me, "Debris—rubbish I am too tired to sweep away myself."

Folding up in a fetal position, I rested for a few minutes while my insides reconstituted themselves. Then we drank cold, sweet well-water out of thick, blue glasses. "Did you hear the great-grandmother?" Namka asked. "Clear as a bell," I replied.

August 22, 1991

This morning my mother called from the hospital to say she has cancer in her lungs and her liver. She sounded resigned, even peaceful, and explained that it's time for her to go. I know that in her aching heart she sees her separation from my father coming to an end.

That end is looming up fast, though, and I'm afraid—for her, for me, and for my unsuspecting three-year-old daughter, who is about to lose her beloved grandmother and dearest friend. Although I can't imagine the world without my mother in it, I hope this part goes fast so she won't have to suffer much.

August 23, 1991

It's 2:30 A.M. and I've just been roused from a restless sleep by the lights flipping on full blast and Sasha sailing into a good-size temper tantrum in the middle of our bedroom. Sasha's not the only one feeling out of sorts. I have a low-grade sore throat and a high level of sadness and dread. Later this morning I'm scheduled to talk to my mom and her doctor about her prognosis. One thing is certain: no longer will I have to worry about her catching a sore throat from me.

Soon there will be only four of us left from this fine old clan of artists, adventurers, film people, dancers, eccentrics, genteel drunks, and lovers of life—my brother Peter, my niece Kris, an aunt, and me. I thank God that I have a child and husband who love me. That love is going to help me put one foot in front of the other over the next few months.

My mother says that for weeks now she has felt someone touching her here and there on her body. Turning, she sees no one, yet she knows who is there: the black-haired, ravishingly handsome, blue-eyed Celt who even in death has not left her. She dreams nightly of him as well, and cannot wait to join him. God, be merciful; let it be quick for this woman I both love and fight with from the bottom of my heart.

A few days after my mother entered the hospital, I started a four-by-six-foot painting of Rain Caller, another character who has recently surfaced. He came with his rattle and his magic while the residents of Tucson all waited for relief from the heat. Rain Caller brought a much needed storm, unleashing the wrath of the gods, and now that the painting is finished and the monsoons are under way, I can hardly think of anything but Mom. I must quickly bring this cycle of work to a close and prepare for the deathwatch.

It's 5:00 A.M. and I can hear the faint *click-click* of Sue, my dad's ancient black Labrador retriever, mincing down the tiled hallways of our desert home looking for my mother. When my father was alive, Sue was always at his left side, fawning against his arthritis-stiffened legs until she fell over in the ecstasy of her adoration. (My father had that effect on females.) She would wait, ears pricked, dark eyes melting, until he surreptitiously slipped her a piece of forbidden coffee cake. Now she is twelve and a half, at least fifteen pounds overweight, and searching through the house for the woman whose side she has rarely left since my father's death.

I remember when Sue was much younger and my parents had just bought a spread on Hat Creek, in Lassen National Forest near the Oregon-California border, where the open country was intoxicating. There Sue and I would hike in the mountains for hours. One day while hiking with Philippe, my first husband, we unsuspectingly walked onto a neighboring cattle ranch, where Sue bounded gleefully into a vicious, ragged-toothed coyote trap. Despite our combined efforts, Philippe and I were unable to pry open the steel jaws of the trap; the more we tried, the more Sue, an exceedingly gentle dog, bit Philippe.

Finally, in horror, I ran as fast as I could to my parents' house about a mile away. I arrived winded, asthmatic, and terrified that my ignorance would result in the crippling of my dad's beloved companion and hunting dog. When Dad and I arrived on the scene in his four-wheel drive, Sue was still firmly ensnared. Suddenly Philippe, with his hands covered in blood from her frantic bites, managed to jimmy the trap open, whereupon Sue leaped free and began bounding wildly in the air like a young antelope. Jumping into the near-freezing creek, she swam about gaily, then sprung out and pursued us, all the while shaking the water out of her coat.

In addition to tough, sweet Sue, there's Bini, our German shepherd, who has given me twelve years of devoted service and companionship, and who now lies draped across my doorway. I have been checking on her every few hours, touching her gently with my foot to see if she, too, has resigned from active service; but she is nearly blind, quite deaf, and so far into the next world that she no longer feels the touch of my foot. The entire epic of the first part of my life is coming to an end; most of the original cast of characters will not be returning for the sequel; and my heart is breaking. Please, God, help me want to stay in the Land of the Living.

August 25, 1991

I spent yesterday morning drumming with Zelima. Beginning to drum is a lot like losing your virginity. For one thing, the questions are the same: Will I be able to do it? Who will show me how? Will I be able to find the beat? Will I look foolish? For another, as soon as the drumming starts, all else is forgotten. You drum from the heart into the pulse of humanity, picking up the never-ending beat of the earth's heart.

Before we started drumming, Zelima spoke for about half an hour as we sipped magenta prickly pear juice sprinkled with a formidable layer of cayenne pepper. Tears rolled relentlessly down my pale cheeks, which was no problem cosmetically, as I have ceased to wear eye makeup. Why should I bother, since within minutes it would all be in my ever-damp bandanna? In any case, it turned out that even in Zelima's presence I could not distance myself from my mother's plight. I thought about the pain, sadness, and flashes of fear that wash over the dear, weary face I am not going to see for much longer.

Zelima spoke of the drumming; the careful listening needed to step into the sound; the skin; the moment. I sweated from the combination of cayenne and grief. From under her altar she pulled out a basket of drums and shakers. I chose my weapon—a wooden nail-keg topped with a stretched skin, which looked like it would fit between my legs. Zelima heated the barrel over the gas jet in her kitchen to make the skin tight and responsive. She then pounded her big flat drum to mark the start of the path, and we set off down an ancient track.

It was an intoxicating journey. As I listened to my heart, succumbed to the pain, and let it out through the drumming, my fingertips burned and sweat mixed with the tears rolling down my face. Soon a message to the spirit world welled up from deep inside me: "Get ready. A great woman is coming." Again and again "A great woman is coming" played through my scorched fingertips.

My first drumming song inspired a host of reflections. Who thought of my mother as great? Many people did. Had she lived an ordinary life? Not at all. An extraordinary beauty and a fine dancer, she fell in love with my equally good-looking dad the day they met. Several months later she learned from a double-page spread in the society section of the *L. A.*

Times that he was married to someone else. By then she was pregnant with my brother. She endured her pregnancy in secret, as befitted a post-Victorian woman with an emotionally abusive father. Then when my brother Peter was over a year old, Dad's wife granted him a divorce, whereupon he joined my mother. People who knew them had low expectations of their union, as it was my father's third marriage.

But like wolves, they mated for life. Throughout decades of drinking, fighting, and making up, they were literally wild about each other. The birth of Peter, who suffered from polio, a rare brittle-bone disease, as well as countless other illnesses, was followed six years later by the arrival of my unhappy sister, Sharon. I was their last child, born eight years afterward.

Two of us were plagued by physical illness. Peter spent most of his childhood alone in hospitals; when he wasn't in bed, he was raised primarily by the emotionally twisted people who produced my mom. At the age of five, I showed signs of serious asthma. I can count on two hands the number of times I went to school five days in a row. Mother believed she was somehow responsible for our physical problems. Who knows why—genetics, anxiety, alcohol and tobacco, or sheer wrath of God.

My mother was noticeably drunk every day as far back as I can remember. During the week, my dad was a highly respected film editor—responsible for such classics as *Magnificent Seven, The Great Escape, Manchurian Candidate,* and *Cat on a Hot Tin Roof,* as well as a string of brooding Clint Eastwood movies—but on weekends he was nearly unrecognizable. Transformed by alcohol, he would spew out endless streams of epithets at my mother, who egged him on. I loved them both, but was terrified by the emotional voltage they generated.

Although my childhood was dominated by the abandonment fears common to the offspring of chronically drunk parents, after years of therapy as well as hundreds of hours spent counseling others, I have concluded that my parents were far better than most. Exhuming the beauty and support they passed on to me was not easy; first, their legacy of fear, self-loathing, and inability to form healthy relationships had to be dynamited out, resulting in jolts of explosive anger and oceans of tears. My parents were simultaneously awful and wonderful—true Hollywood eccentrics—and I would not trade them for anyone in the world.

In preparing for the end of my mother's life on this plane, I have a different perspective from when I was younger and righteously outraged. My mother came from a family far more toxic than mine, and her dad brutalized her; therapy was unavailable to her; and people of her generation were discouraged from talking about their needs, their fears, or their pain. Yet despite these handicaps, my mother was always tender with me. She enrolled me in my first art classes, paid for my art supplies and lessons until I was married, insisted that I paint rather than get a "regular" job, paid for my nontraditional dance lessons that emphasized joy of movement and expression of feeling in lieu of steps or recitals, and in general treated me as if I were a goddess of the arts.

She knew how important movement and music were to the human soul, and she also knew I was destined to be an artist. Yet unlike her father, who had forced her into the life of a child star, she never pushed me; she simply provided the atmosphere and means for fulfilling that destiny.

Moreover, she often told me I was beautiful, inside and out. Many people were beautiful on the outside, she would say, but what was inside me was exceptional. How I wished she could have seen this quality in herself! And then there were the terrifying drunken fights and vicious name-calling—sources of the enormous pain that compelled me to express myself creatively.

Although I have felt trapped while taking care of my mother, I am grateful to have spent her last few years with her. I have no regrets; there is nothing I should have done that I didn't do, nothing to come back to haunt me. Great Spirit, stay with her. Stay with me too.

August 31, 1991

It has been raining since yesterday, and the desert earth is giving off a warm, sensuous smell. The red ants and legions of wild critters we usually see out the bedroom window are hiding, perhaps huddling under giant palo verdes that blanket the land. Tarantulas will soon come marching out, as they often do after a rainstorm. That's when you have to be careful opening doors to the desert, since the rascals just might scoot in determinedly. If they do, you had better be ready with your hockey stick, because they move *fast*.

In the midst of yesterday's rain Mom, weak and shaky, came home from the hospital with a request: she wanted to see Sasha christened. Although I personally didn't think my three year old needed it, since the radiance of her spirit is apparent to anyone in her presence, we arranged for David, the minister at Saint Francis Church, to come christen her. When he arrived, Sasha liked him and even invited him to play, but wanted nothing to do with the baptismal water, which Sue was by then slurping out of the bowl. At the mere mention of the ceremony, Sasha barked like a dog and ran down the hall. No amount of pleading, explaining, or commanding could change her mind.

David, persevering nonetheless, sat on the floor in the living room with Sasha and "baptized" eight of her stuffed animals and dolls. He blessed two bunnies, two Snoopys, Kitty, Pony, Armadillo, and her baby doll Cassie, who had to be wrapped to stop leaking. But no way was he was going to baptize our little wild child.

With regret about my inability to fulfill one of my mother's last requests, I went to her room to tell her there was not going to be a christening. Before I said a word, my mother wistfully confided in me that she herself had never been christened since no one in her family had cared enough about her to do it. She went on to say that she wasn't seen as valuable until her twisted father began turning her into a money-making property—which is why she had us kids go through the ceremonial consignment into the hands of God even though we weren't churchgoers.

Astonished by this revelation, I asked if she would like David to christen her. Yes, she would like that, she replied. I couldn't remember her requesting anything other than another glass of wine in all the years I knew her; to the contrary, all her life she had given herself away in large chunks.

Moments later Bob, David, Sasha, and I gathered in my mother's room for her baptism. A photograph of my father looked down at us all as David asked us to hold hands, spoke a few words, and then sprinkled several drops of water on Mom's tired old head. Peacefulness reigned during the baptism of this very spiritual nonreligious woman on the brink of death.

It seemed fitting to hold this sacred send-off—like cracking a champagne bottle on a ship about to cross the sea. To accentuate the celebratory nature of the occasion, Sasha opened a pink plastic bottle of soapy liquid, and proceeded to fill the room with what David called "baptismal bubbles."

As it turned out, yesterday was one of the most important days in my mother's life. She came home to die and was washed clean of the grime of a lifetime for her upcoming journey. It was an important day for me too. I was there for my mother's baptism—her initiation into another life.

When night fell, I told my mother I had written a book; it was the one thing I thought I might regret not saying to her before she dies. She was simultaneously surprised and composed. "I always knew you were great," she replied, looking deeply into my eyes. Telling my mother about *Warrior Woman* was like ceremonially entering the next phase of my life.

September 2, 1991

It's about 6:30 A.M. and the nurse we have hired to watch my mother is by her side, allowing Bob and me a few moments of rest. The house reeks of urine, excrement, cancer, and death.

Last night, after trying to clean up some of my mother's leakage, I entered the soft darkness of the desert, only to find the death smell clinging darkly to my shirt and unwashed hair. I returned home and showered, only to discover that this smell can't be washed off, though water does temporarily smooth out crawly skin.

Then this morning at 5:00, I lay wide awake listening to my mother's groans and soon realized that the best thing I could do for myself was step quietly into my office and record my thoughts and feelings. With my heart torn to pieces, I can't paint; yet words come, and plenty of emotions too. Having this expressive outlet, I don't feel completely obliterated.

Interestingly, it's hard to stay quiet even long enough to pray, but when I open myself to writing, I am linked directly to the great source, and the palliative effects are immediate. Now I know there are many alternative ways to pray when it's raining shit.

Praying is what I've been doing most—not only for my mother but for Bini, my loving four-legged companion. Yesterday morning she looked quite low, and I spent hours giving her sips of water from a small bowl I held up to her muzzle. At midday, when her life energy seemed to be evaporating, I began a telephone quest for a veterinarian who would make a house call, since we can't leave my mother alone now. I finally found a horse vet who said she could come when we needed her.

Toward evening, as I looked into Bini's eyes, I knew it was time for her to leave me. But I couldn't let her die alone and outside in the dark while I tended to Mom. Nor could the equine vet come at this hour because, as it turned out, she had two emergencies to take of. It became apparent that I was going to have to either take my old friend to an emergency clinic or muster up the courage to "do" her myself. The latter option proved nonviable, since Mom's pain had sent her into a world somewhat brightened by massive doses of morphine and we were not willing to spare the drugs. There comes a time when you have to choose who gets the nursing and the drugs.

With an overwhelming sense of nausea, Bob and I wrapped Bini in blankets and loaded her into the van. While he stayed home with Mom, I drove off to the emergency clinic wailing aloud in pain. Once there, I parked, helped the attendant carry Bini in on a doggie stretcher, and although barely articulate, arranged for her to be put down. Then I said a final good-bye to my loyal friend and gave her a kiss.

To preserve what little energy I had, I made a survivor's decision not to watch Bini die. Sobbing uncontrollably, I retired to the waiting room, where I remained until they told me she was gone. Then I bolted out the door howling, which caused concern among the pool-hall denizens who shared the parking lot with the clinic's clientele.

On the way home I involuntarily emitted noises of grief from an animal part of myself as my stark fear of losing my mother tangoed with the pain of missing my loyal friend. Then suddenly, I noticed that Bini was sitting in the passenger seat. Quick as could be, she had transmuted into a spirit dog! Although I could see through her, there she was—the strong, fierce dog-ninja she had been in her prime, after a year of strenuous training. Her ears were pricked, her eyes alert and forward, her profile noble. To take me through my hardest transition, she'd had to leave her old worn-out body behind.

Not only was this great spirit dog holding back my collapse and giving me courage, but she was leading a *pack* of spirit dogs! Through Bini's transparency I could see my former canine guardians: Rover, the golden retriever who appointed himself my guardian angel and refused to allow the baby-sitter near me when my parents left the house; Arky, the blind mind-reading black Labrador who threatened anyone smelling of danger; Bill, another black Labrador, who hanged herself on her collar while trying to come home from a kennel she was boarding in; Traps and Maggie, also Labs, my family's longtime hunting dogs; Toucan, the feisty Welsh corgi who liked to bark; Nando, the hellish German shepherd with whom I fell in love; and Bella, the beauteous Doberman. I took comfort in the appearance of my old friends.

Then Bini spoke: "I am protecting you in the other world now. If anyone comes to hurt you in the everyday world, I will attack them in the spirit world, and an attack in the spirit world is far more devastating than anything you are capable of imagining—the victim is not able to recover. Rest . . . I will guard you while you sleep."

Within minutes of returning home, I fell asleep for several hours before resuming the vigil with my mother. Even then I felt Bini close to me. Like the desert wind, which also cannot be seen, her presence is powerful. Her love has not left me; only her old worn-out body has.

September 3, 1991

My mother is now using a potty chair and wearing adult diapers, which I change for her. Seeing one's mother revert to diapers is almost more than a human being can bear, and yet in life we cycle through the birth and death process again and again. For now, I am consoled by this cycling notion, and I am more certain than ever that Mom will soon choose to leave.

September 4, 1991

Mom has made her decision and moved into what appear to be the final hours of her life. About an hour ago, we toasted each other good-bye in a fleeting moment of interlinked consciousness—me with a glass of water, her with a morphine cocktail—as she proclaimed, *"Salud, amor, y pesetas, y el tiempo para gustarlos."* ("Health, love, wealth, and the time to enjoy them.")

Her appearance has already changed. She is wearing the face of death, with her upper lip curved down and pulled far over her top teeth now rotten from steroids. Everything that needs to be said between us has been said. She is sailing out peacefully—bride of the departed Celtic warrior, slipping out to join him in a small silvery boat of morphine dreams. I kissed her good-bye.

The awful stench has left, and I am able to nuzzle against her. Lifting her limp arm, I ran her inert yet still warm fingers through my hair for fresh cellular memories of the touch of her beautiful hands on my head. No longer can she hold me as she did three days ago when I returned from taking Bini to the emergency clinic and she whispered, "I am so sorry this is happening now. I am sorry to be leaving you. This is going to be a horrible birthday for you," an occasion that she somehow knew was just over two weeks away.

Sasha came in periodically to rest her head on her grandma's chest and to kiss her on the cheek. Bob stepped in, too, tenderly rubbing her feet for long periods of time. I see her relationship with Bob as a means of coming to terms with her painful feelings toward my brother.

September 6, 1991

Mom died at 5:30 this morning. Bob and I had gone to bed four and a half hours earlier, sick with exhaustion from the death vigil, and had somehow managed to sleep through her moment of transition.

I do not feel bad about not being there at the very end. One reason is that at some point survivors have to tend to the living rather than sacrifice the family's well-being to the dying. Another is that Mom was well attended. A nurse named Sharon—an angel in human form—had been reading the Bible to herself at Mom's side when she died. There had been a deep bond between them, and I am certain God sent this loving soul to be with her when she died.

The morning seemed empty. I felt the loss of someone who knew me and loved me. Who, I wondered, can possibly want to know me as a loving mother wants to know her child?

The afternoon brought a strange form of consolation. While walking in the desert, I had the frightening sensation that I had been lifted off the ground. In this floating state I received a powerful message: "You have come to the end of the road with your parents, and you were a good daughter."

Being a good daughter, I realized, had been part of my life path. Even as a child I wanted to ease my parents' pain and chase away the demons that kept sending them to the bottle. My assignment was to know them and love them—which I did. That task is over now as my mother joins the river of women who will mother me from beyond this plane.

September 8, 1993

Sue, the black Labrador, has been holed up in Mom's room for two and a half days. Agonizing over the loss of her master and mistress, she's starving herself to death and peeing all over the carpet. Although I had thought she would live a few more years, I must take her to the veterinarian today and let this poor creature join Bini and Mom. It would be cruel to force her to stay alive so I won't have to grieve another loss.

In eight days I will be forty years old. For more reasons than chronology alone, my young womanhood has drawn to a close.

Chapter 4

Initiation

Tucson, Arizona
September 18, 1991

It's 1:00 A.M. and I'm ragged with exhaustion. Like a child who has gone too long without a nap, I have pushed myself way past the point of relaxing into a healing sleep. Twenty minutes ago, as I stood quietly in the dark kitchen steeping a soporific witch's brew, I heard a high-pitched squeak from a bat as it careened swiftly past the open window.

The primitive sound, hitting some obscure memory button, sent me back to the day after my mother's death. I had just given Sasha a set of washable marking pens and was sitting in our flower-filled courtyard with my friend Heidi. Suddenly, Sasha joined us, naked as a little pink shrimp, and began to make large slash marks all over her body with the red marker. The effect was jarring, tribal, unsettling. Perhaps, I thought, unconscious memories from other lifetimes have prompted her to resort to this ancient ritualistic expression of her grief, to create this primitive outward sign of abject mourning.

Sasha's grieving has been gut-wrenching. The tearing and ripping taking place inside her comes out in the most unnerving tantrums I have ever seen her have. Her pain is so palpable and unstoppable that I am certain she senses the loss of her grandmother is tremendous, both for herself and for her mother. When Mom's not okay, Sasha knows it.

Concerned that much of her emotionality stems from her connection to me and that my grief has become too great for her to witness, I recently decided to pull the reins in on it—at least when I am with her. Since then, I have stabilized greatly during the day, although I am unable to sleep well at night.

Yesterday, eager to bring new life into the family, Bob, Sasha, and I piled into our van and drove to California to pick up two German shepherds from a primo trainer named Dean Calderon. Brujo, age two, and Bella II, age one and a half, joined the tribe officially last night, but there was no sleeping with the uncivilized beasts in our boudoir. Tonight they are in their crates, yet sleep continues to elude me.

And so does the desire to paint. Propped up on my easel is a sketch of Crow Woman who came during my last "night flight" with Namka back in July, before all the dying started. I have no drive to paint this image because I feel cut off from channels that hook me up to the source. Maybe students will come now that I have time for them. If I had students to attend to, I'd get into the studio, and once there, I'd know how to begin: gaze at the blank canvas, pick up the brush . . . This is what will hook me back up to the source.

I'm up late, not only because I am unable to sleep and beset by grief but also because I've got the willies. Several times over the past few hours I've used the bathroom adjoining my mom's old room, and each time I've been frightened to open the door; then upon returning to my office, I've been scared that someone is standing behind me. The mere movement of air through the ceiling fan sends tremors of animal fear through me. My hunch is not that these sensations are emanating from the entity my mother has become, but rather that my deep grief has left me momentarily unprotected against whatever cosmic trash is leaking from the room down the hall and whatever malevolent being is watching me through the crack in the door behind me. I've got to slam down the hatches and get out of here right now. This is not the sort of energy I want to hook up to!

September 21, 1991

Having awakened in one of my wired states, I'm in my office serving as a net in a tennis game between our two insolent black cats and the dark-muzzled wolf dog named Bella. She is too young to know office etiquette: no predation, no fights, no roughhousing, no eating of art supplies or favorite pens, no barfing, and no shitting. Based on Bella's proclivities, it is time to add "no nibbling on socks." The positive rules are less numerous: stay in the room, lie down and make yourself invisible, catch all living leftovers from the cats' hunting sprees, bark at the bad guys.

My window is open to the night air, reminding me that it's autumn here in Tucson. Although the days are still warm, the light has turned golden and falls more obliquely than before, and the desert nights bring an unmistakable coolness. I love autumn in my hacienda.

Even so, I miss the intimacy of Santa Fe, though less acutely than I did six months ago. When I lived in that city of smaller scale, the perimeters of my world were more harmonious with my temperament. Because I arrived in Santa Fe knowing no one but Bob, while residing there we came to know each other in the same way two countrymen come to know each other while living abroad. We were forced to talk about everything, to stretch, to grow fast like chamisa in the spring. There we surrendered, fell in love, married, and gave birth to an angel. How can I not miss a place so ripe with meaning?

September 22, 1991

It's a full moon night and I am wide awake, ragged from aftereffects of the enormous overdoses of adrenaline surging through me as a result of the protracted stress over my mother's death. The good news is that I sold one of my easels to a woman and have made arrangements for her to come paint with me for an hour and a half tomorrow morning. It's not so much a lesson as a strategy to get myself painting.

My plan is to work on the image of Crow Woman. I would also like to paint Skeleton Woman, the herald of death and transformation that came riding on her horse of bones out of a fire. When energy is at a premium, it is often easier to work on one very large image, which is how I envision this figure of bones. If I hold back, conserving my intensity just a little, I know I'll be able to capture her powerful essence. All that is needed is the time it takes to get the horse on the bit; then as the reins are loosened, the formidable strength and speed of the wild horse will play its part.

A buyer for "Skull on Turquoise," painted last May, came to dinner tonight and left with the canvas. I felt good watching it go, although I will miss it. Seeing the bare spot on the adobe brick wall was even better. Bare walls are my greatest inspiration!

Also inspiring is my new office, where I am now sitting. It's the nice big room that used to be my mother's bedroom. We had it painted ultra-white, changed the carpets, then moved in all my furniture, including a single bed to stretch out on. Hanging from the wall behind the bed is a sun-bleached white skull; on an adjacent wall is the four-by-five-foot "Soft Rocks"; and over the closet door is the four-by-six-foot "Rain Caller." All in all, the turquoise, purple, and bottle-greens of the room are soothing and inviting.

While peering out the front window of my new office before turning on the lights, I saw Indian fig, Spanish bayonet, prickly pear, and barrel cactus all lit in the chromium wash of the full moon. It felt as if everything in the silver-dusted desert had been dancing with abandon and had lurched to a halt in slightly unnatural poses when I stepped to the window. On full moon nights the desert takes on the appearance of a dreamscape.

As I flipped on the lights, I remembered we had plans to hike up Mount Lemmon with the new dogs later this week. I'm thinking of taking Mom's and Dad's ashes with us so we can scatter them. Right now they are in two small boxes on my turquoise bookcase. Mom's moccasins are resting on top of Dad's box of ashes, and the watch he wore every day for over thirty years is on top of her box. The watch—a gift to him from Mom—had an alarm that my sister and I would sabotage on school mornings.

September 27, 1991

This week I painted! As I had hoped, the woman who came to my studio provided just the impetus I needed to get going. She is in her late thirties, has a one-and-a-half-year-old child, and hasn't had the energy to paint since her pregnancy. Excited at the prospect of having a guest, I started painting an hour before her arrival. The image came out clean and fast, and was nearly finished by the time the woman appeared.

The image I worked with was Crow Woman. Her face is so androgynous-looking that Bob thought she was a man. I like this mutable aspect of my paintings, because it allows viewers to see whatever is meaningful to them, and it enables me to find whatever I am seeking as well, which often changes over time. We all see what we need to see.

"Crow Woman," I must say, is a grand painting. When I started out, I set low standards for myself, striving only to get painting—not to complete the work, and certainly not to produce a masterpiece. All the crying and letting go I have done these three weeks must have flooded out major blockages, for there wasn't much of me left to get in my own way. Afterward, exhilarated by a new sense of momentum, I called the stretcher-bar wholesaler to order canvas makings for a five-by-six-foot painting of Skeleton Woman.

October 5, 1991

This afternoon someone asked me if it felt strange to think that following the release of *Warrior Woman,* people all over the galaxy were going to know me intimately. "No," I replied, "they will be reading about another woman." And it is true—I am growing and changing at such great speed that what I wrote as recently as six months ago has little to do with who I am now. People who read my book will be tracking shadows on a wall days after the dancers are gone. In fact, I am already long down the road to my next destination.

October 8, 1991

It's now 5:15 A.M. and I've been writing for two hours, keenly aware that this pattern is tied to some strange *need* to work in the very early morning. As the years go by, I'm less inclined to resist these promptings, but I bounce back more crookedly from the lack of deep sleep. If I could wake up to write at 5:00 A.M., instead of 2:00 A.M. or 3:00 A.M., I would go to sleep earlier in the evening. But no—the writing process seems intertwined with my dream cycles and there's no changing it.

The dogs seem to understand this idiosyncrasy. I spent the night in my new office with Bella, the little female German shepherd who has become my shadow. As we retired, Brujo moved quietly down the hall to guard the rest of the family.

Now I see that the sky out the window has taken on a mauve color, and the light is changing rapidly, adding a promising rosiness to the palette. The chollas are a shiny silver in the predawn light. I cherish my solitude—perhaps that is my gift from the night work.

November 4, 1991

I've just returned from giving a week-long workshop in Mazatlán, in western Mexico. At the start of the week, I was worried that I had nothing to offer, that I wouldn't be able to crank up the juices of creativity so soon after my mother's death, that I would merely disintegrate—none of which could have been further from the truth. When I felt like crying, I cried, deep and long, regardless of the focus of our session. Moreover, I participated actively in the sessions. If the work is good enough for attendees, I figured, it's good enough for me.

And indeed it was. The writing dislodged gallons of tears. The movement cracked loose feelings and memories long stuck in my body. My artwork was filled with mystical pictures from my childhood and adobe houses in the foothills of the Sangre de Cristo Mountains of New Mexico. I cried as much over my memory of adobes as over the loss of my parents.

Now that I'm back, I cannot drag myself to my desk. I don't want to pay the bills, or face the stack of letters that have been stagnating there since our arrival from Kingman. I certainly have no desire to tackle the guilt-inducing piles of notes and telephone messages. "Get to the pink utility bills before they disconnect us," I've been telling myself, "and throw the rest in the trash."

It is at times like this that I need my mother most. I want to hear her voice on the phone, or better yet, walk down the hall and visit her. Actually, I want to curl up in her arms and feel her holding me.

At times like this I also know my creative energy is bottled up and in need of an outlet. I have an excellent image to work with—this woman of bones—but almost no drive to stretch the canvas for it. Nevertheless, she will probably be painted soon, since I feel another wave of pain rising up to propel me forward, like the swell of the tide before a wave breaks. My commitment for the next few days will have to be scaled down to simply stretching the canvas.

November 5, 1991

Everything is stuck! I have owls flying around my consciousness, skeletal women on horseback tramping through its central layer, and not the slightest desire to paint. I'll have to cut my goals back another notch—to setting up on the easel a twenty-four-by-thirty-inch blank canvas and just looking at. I'm also going to call the office at Saint Francis Church to see about arranging for an ARTS meeting. These two courses of action are sure to relieve my constipated creativity.

November 13, 1991

Such strange goings-on have been flickering inside me that I have hesitated to write about my current mental state. About ten days ago I quit taking birth control pills, out of a simple desire to go *au naturel* for a while; and now I am either undergoing early menopause or experiencing severe hormonal surges with acute PMS-like mood swings and hot flashes.

Furthermore, I am suffering from severe missing-of-the-mother. I long to have a heart-to-heart with her. I feel as if there is no safe place in all the world for me to lay down my burdens and worries. In addition, I've been seriously at odds with Bob these past few days and unable to find the pickax needed to shatter the wall between us.

These disturbances in my personal life engulf me, particularly the breakdown in communication with Bob. Each time I try to talk with him, he seems to slip farther away from me. Although we probably need hours of marathon talks, neither of us is currently interested in long discussions. We're at one of those crossroads where a couple either chooses to grow closer together or succumbs to a parting of the ways. In long-term relationships such junctures are approached again and again—never at a convenient time. And never without fear.

In the studio, things are clearer. After much straining, I have managed to put a blank canvas up in preparation for Tecolote, the Owl—a piece commissioned by a local businesswoman. First, however, I completed a study in oil of a big skull I recently bought from a local curio dealer. What an inspiring piece of animal anatomy this forty-eight-inch-tall Watusi skull is; it's three times the size of an ordinary cow skull, with colossal horns like spikes a sculptor might have chiseled from stone. God is a great artist!

My current goal is to get out the stretcher bars for the big painting of the skeleton emerging from fire on her horse of bones. Sometimes I see a pack of skeleton hounds racing alongside her, and I know they are the spirit dogs that follow me everywhere in both my waking and dream worlds. Although in the house of spirits they play like wild dogs, I don't think I'll clutter up the painting with this carnival of animals; simple seems better.

November 18, 1991

After performing every procrastination trick possible, I have managed to assemble the stretcher bars for a five-by-six-foot painting. It must be a very loaded painting for me—at least that is the thought that keeps pushing me through my inertia. The truth is that I *know* this piece will mark a major transition in my life. This painting is going to change me.

Now that the stretcher bars are assembled, it is time to lock up the canine terrorists and bring in the roll of oversized canvas. Whereas some artists love to stretch their canvases, I'd much prefer to spend every ounce of my creative energy ripping out images. While operating out of my Los Angeles studio, I would simply phone my supplier and ask him to deliver a truckload of already stretched canvases. Here in Tucson, however, no such luxury exists, because not many people stretch canvases for a reasonable fee.

In addition to assembling the stretcher bars, I've taken another step forward: I've arranged for an ARTS meeting to be held at the church next week. This gathering is likely to provide the shot of energy I need as a result of the holocaust in my home. I want to refocus on my creativity. I want to push more out of myself while I'm filled with passion. I want to paint this Skeleton Woman while she is smoldering.

As for this week, I will be resuming my work with Zelima. I dream about her frequently and look forward to the stimulation she will no doubt provide. In addition, I've started to put Sasha to bed at 8:00 in the evening, instead of 9:00 or 9:30. This change alone has freed up a large chunk of time and energy for my work and for attending to my own needs.

November 30, 1991

This has been a busy week, inside and out. The day before yesterday was Thanksgiving—my first without my mother and a strangely quiet occasion. I didn't miss her, which at the outset seemed odd. Then I flashed back on last Thanksgiving, when we were in Kingman. Bob, Sasha, and I had gone for a holiday walk to a neighbor's home while our houseguest Larry stayed behind and baby-sat a roasting turkey. On our return walk, we heard sirens in the distance. Immediately, I began racing through the desert, trying to beat the fire truck and ambulance that I somehow knew were en route to our house. My mother, it turned out, had fallen off the toilet, breaking ribs and spilling blood all over the bathroom. Leaving Larry with instructions for basting the turkey, I accompanied Mom on her ambulance ride to the hospital. Although she recovered rather quickly from that incident, I am only now recuperating from years spent in a state of ever-ready vigilance.

Yesterday I joined the Thursday night women's group at a rented cabin on Mount Lemmon for a post-Thanksgiving gathering. At one point in the afternoon, we shared thoughts about what we were thankful for. When my turn came, I said that I was thankful my mother was dead, that an illness any more prolonged would have been unbearably inhumane.

I returned home horrified to have said such a thing. Stepping out into the freezing Tucson night, I called out to her: "Forgive me, Mom, for sometimes being glad that you are dead. It certainly seems better than watching you rot in some nursing home. I couldn't have stood seeing you come to that, you once wild woman. Do people ask real friends to come back from the dead? If so, I wish you could come back and talk to me, hold me, comfort me, mother me, if only for a few minutes. Where did your love for me go when your body died? Why can't I feel it? How does a woman live in this big scary world without a mother loving her?" I fell asleep feeling that I had lost a dear friend and would never see her again.

Before Thanksgiving, my world looked brighter. For one thing, my book was released! I couldn't believe what I was seeing when I opened the box from the printer—my cover painting, my title, my words. The publication of a book brings all the amazement of a birth experience, yet a book, unlike a baby, ushers in a feeling of completion. Am I, like many other first-time authors, fearful that I may never write again? No, because the words keep pouring out. All I have to do is step aside and out they flow.

Another high point of the week was our first ARTS meeting, held on Monday. Five of us were present, and for me it was a glorious reentry into life. We talked about our creativity—free of judgments, blame, and preachy lectures. At the end of the meeting, we went around the room and made a commitment to our art for the coming week. I said I would drag my big canvas, which I finally did stretch, onto the easel so I could look at it. Gazing at a big white empty expanse of canvas always activates my "internal slide projector."

Although Skeleton Woman is very charged for me, I won't understand her true importance until I paint her. What I do understand is this: the painting is about my initiation into a new life, and it's packed with emotional gunpowder.

Chapter 5

Skeleton Woman

Tucson, Arizona
December 2, 1991

Sasha went to sleep at her new bedtime of 8:00 P.M., and I am glad to be working in my purple, turquoise, and green office. I am trying not to discharge my need to write by getting trapped in long, draining phone conversations. Recently, my life has filled up with people, leaving me precious little time to be quiet and listen to myself.

The giant canvas for Skeleton Woman stares at me blankly in the studio. Before I go to sleep tonight, I'll dig out the original sketch and look at it. Staring at a sketch I like often incubates a painting.

Then tomorrow, I'll get out my little black book and do another drawing of Skeleton Woman, maybe even let her talk a bit. Since I haven't been painting with regularity, I need a transitional activity like sketching to "prime the pump" and get my momentum going.

December 5, 1991

The energy I feel while writing this journal is entirely new to me. While writing my first book, I was much more patient, and appreciative of every effort I put forth as an artist. As my life went through wrenching changes every few months, I simply paddled along, making notes on small pieces of paper and shoving them in my field bag or coat pocket, or behind the visor in my car. Before taking up residence in my truck midway through the 1980s—when I spent a year traveling through the badlands of California, Arizona, and New Mexico with my paints and my dog Chile—I had no thought of recording my experiences in entire paragraphs. Then years later, when I had access to a computer, I dug through those dusty old pockets for little pieces of crumpled paper to string my life together. Actually, I was looking to see if it *could* be strung together!

Now I feel compelled to tell my story, for it pushes at me steadily. Every few days, while poised at the computer or my writing pad, I pull more octopuses out of the dark recesses of my plumbing. These old critters, together with the events of my present life—many of which send me spiraling inward for refuge—serve as inspiration for my art. The point is this: *nothing that takes place in my life is separate from my art.* If I were to stop painting every time the going gets rough, I would never complete a canvas.

One of the most beautiful aspects of writing is the potential words have of reaching people around the world. In response to *Warrior Woman,* for example, readers from far corners of the globe send letters telling me they are doing their writing and painting, playing the saxophone, lifting their heads and singing again. Acetylene torches are firing up in concrete jungles, and giant puppets are rearing up their phosphorescent heads at twilight, shimmering to the sluttish smash and clang of trash-can drums. The world is vibrant with the chanting, stamping, and drumming—the coming back to life of creative people who are tuning into their own kinky radio stations. Folks are screaming and crying and raging and making love and poetry and getting all this down on paper and canvas for the uplifting of the human spirit everywhere. Each day, more people are getting up to join the conga line.

If sufficient time and resources were available, I'd send every letter writer a postcard saying: "I can't write back to you—I'm too busy dancing. I'm thrilled that you took time to write, but mostly I'm thrilled that you're making your art. Keep right on doing all those things they tell you cannot be done!"

I'm getting ready to write a few magazine articles about my mother's dying. It might have been easier to compose them closer to her death, but at the time, I could barely put together a meal or remember to breathe. Then after the grieving came a strong pull to run from the memories, the pain, and the missing. Now I feel a strenuous repression plugging up my work, keeping me from the big blank canvas that's yelling for paint. And although I dread writing the articles, doing so is sure to clear the residue of grief from the pipes.

December 8, 1991

I'm sitting at my desk admiring the rain as it falls on my office window. Rain never used to hit the window, because the drops were deflected by a dark blue canvas awning overhead. Then Garth came and not only ripped it down but, to prevent heat buildup in the summer, crafted an exquisite *ramada* out of *latillas*—semistraight peeled-and-split poles. Now that the awning is gone, I can see the Indian fig that towers perhaps twelve feet above the house, as well as saguaros, prickly pears that form an uninviting fence around the house, barrel cactus, Spanish bayonet, yuccas, palo verde trees, and mesquites. They're all here in the room with me.

Two days ago, after stumbling upon a rare block of time alone, I made some frightfully expensive jasmine tea, brought it into my office, and sat down to write an article for *Athena* magazine about the passing of my mother. Before I could finish, though, I had to stop for a really good cry. There are always more tears.

After unleashing the pent-up river, I tied up the loose ends of my article, went to the studio, and began sloshing red paint onto the giant empty canvas. Climbing a five-foot ladder, I applied red paint all the way to the top of the canvas. By then, Sasha had returned and plunked herself on the floor to make reindeer out of brown paper bags. After I had been up and down the ladder several dozen times, Sasha climbed up and played reindeer puppets with me while I painted the lower half of the canvas with my nonpuppet hand. Now at last, the canvas has a layer of paint on it. It's very red.

With the release of all those blocked-up tears, I not only was able to paint but was awakened to the red in my world. Yesterday, while driving home over the ridge that leads to our house, I was struck by the deep blood-red color of the sky. A silhouette of the mountains stood black against the sunset, and the thinnest toenail sliver of a new moon hung low on the skyline. I pulled off to the side of the road again and again to drink in the impossibly red and haunting evening sky.

December 9, 1991

A creative zigzag has me working with singleness of vision for days on end, whereas at other times, four weeks might pass before I'd notice that someone had walked off with all my supplies. Whichever course I'm on arouses concern. When I am in an emotionally agitated state, all I want to do is find relief, by either crying or having a long talk with a friend. When I am working steadily, I worry about myself like a mother fretting over her oddly behaving child, wondering: What's going on with her? Does she have a fever? Is something bothering her? Is she working too hard? Will she explode? Will that ruin the wallpaper?

Currently in the grip of the low-grade anxiety that accompanies heavy artistic binges, I am concerned not only about myself but also about my daughter. At this moment Sasha, who is rapidly approaching the age of four, is watching cartoons on TV. The mess that most broadcasting networks try to pass off as human experience and emotion infuriates me, as do the devaluing ads placed strategically at the most viewer-vulnerable intervals. The amount of money spent on TV programming, as opposed to other art forms, makes me seethe even more. When I become overwrought on this subject, I remind myself that the cartoons boring their way into Sasha's head free me up to complete work from time to time, and that although I as a child spent hours each day as well as long sleepless nights watching TV, my imagination was not stunted; nor did I grow into a "watcher" rather than a "doer."

Any media fears that linger usually vanish when Sasha and I converse. Earlier this morning, for instance, we were having a cup of tea together when she solemnly told me that boogers make her big and strong. "Is there anything more you can tell me about boogers?" I asked. "They're not pretty like nail polish," she replied.

December 14, 1991

Today, like most days, it took quite a bit of maneuvering before I could get to work. First I fed dozens of birds—a welcome legacy handed down by the previous owners of the house. Then I fed the dogs and, because Bella's in heat, strapped a doggie sanitary napkin on her. Next I force-fed the cat and made myself a cup of hot tea. Finally noticing how ungodly quiet it was in our hacienda, I sneaked into Sasha's bathroom and found that she had covered her baby doll, Brujo, a good part of the sink, and herself with a thick layer of Desitin—enough to "keep away any diaper rash" for months! After shoveling off as much as we could, we concluded that a shower was in order.

En route to my office, I saw that the big red canvas was burning up the living room. When I turn into the driveway, I can see the red on fire through the front window, too, sending scarlet clear out to the dusty road we live on. This saturation of red is highly energizing and seems to be warming me back to life.

Two days ago a fresh package of red paint arrived from Santa Fe. I use some colors by Winsor & Newton, an easy brand to find locally, but mostly I favor a French product that must be shipped from either Santa Fe or Atlanta. Remember, no matter what your art teachers say, some shades cannot be whipped up on a palette from your trusty primary colors.

All in all, what's happening in the studio is vibrating throughout the house. I've been applying numerous coats of red paint for depth of color and a certain agitation of the surface. The result is a canvas beautiful enough to hang just as it is. The red is an entity unto itself.

Wind is rushing furiously over the foothills, down through the cactus groves, and into the city of Tucson. This wind, which came up during the night, reminds me of a favorite lover who shows up unexpectedly from Italy—or of my husband, who has now become lover, roots, and passion. I live with a man who is always someone different. He, in turn, lives with Changing Woman, a transformer who is sometimes a panther or a snake, or suddenly a coyote. Varying our personae keeps us from getting bored.

When Bob and I were newlyweds, a friend asked me for the body count in Bob's marriage-go-round. "I am the seventh Mrs. Earll," I replied. Immediately, I reflected back on my first marriage and my certainty that it, too, would last forever. "I suppose Bob and I have about as good a chance as any to survive," I added, realizing how much work such survival takes. We have been together now about five years, and it feels as if we are just getting to know each other.

I'm sitting here trancing out, staring in an unfocused way into the desert. Does a part of me know something that the rest doesn't? Is a catastrophe lurking around the next bend in the road? Most of my family of origin is dead. What am I still doing here?

Such questions are unnerving. Fearful that a vigorous surge in my creative drive might signify the end of my life, I often succumb to an inner voice that says: "So don't create anything. Don't breathe or move a muscle. Spread a blanket over that radiant life force—death won't notice the quivering lump under the blanket. Throw a bridle on that horse and get it into the corral. Slow down. Get down. Lie flat and be quiet. Become invisible."

December 15, 1991

In preparation for the painting of Skeleton Woman, I've borrowed Heidi's elegant horse, Gaugin. There is nothing like being on the back of a spirited horse. Ride the horse before you paint it; eat the still life when the painting is finished. These are two important lessons in art.

I've also renewed a library book I checked out last month portraying a skeletal horse. The librarian who first showed me the volume explained apologetically, "It's kind of amateurish—almost a kid's book on drawing horses." I checked it out right away. Why? Because it's difficult to find horses running around with no meat on them.

December 16, 1991

I've started to paint Skeleton Woman. While the background was burning in the studio, I was expectantly waiting for the rider to materialize, and now she has begun to—one bone at a time. First, however, her horse had to be adjusted. When I had most of the creature painted,

I realized it was positioned too far to the left, so I reluctantly wiped off all the work I had done on him.

The only way to perform this type of surgery without an anesthetic is *quickly,* which is exactly how I proceeded. Because all the background paint had dried, it was like erasing a chalkboard instead of dissolving everything into a torrent of pink. It did not take long to repaint the horse, which now stands better on the canvas.

December 17, 1991

It's 4:30 A.M. and I'm reliving a myriad of scenarios I'd prefer not to think about. For example, I'm replaying yesterday's wake-up scene: "Daddy, there's a mouse in the house!" Although I don't happen to mind mice, waking up to such a proclamation can be disconcerting. My first thoughts were: Where? Running or dead? Big or little? What did its tail look like—bare or furry?

Having once cohabited with an extraordinary feline huntress named Birdie, whose predilection was to bring her prey into my bed and proceed to kill them on top of me while I slept in blessed ignorance of it all, the thought of awakening to partially digested mouse parts—like the memory of awakening to bird feathers on my pillow, under my eyelids, and in my mouth—is daunting. I wanted to know if I would need slippers or rubber boots, a broom or a hockey stick. Was there foam around its mouth? How many of our animals who are now slathering me with kisses have been playing beanbag with the thing?

Bob got up to address the matter. I, meanwhile, realizing why Puma, our formidable hunter, lay exhausted at the foot of the bed, tiptoed out to see his handiwork. Nestled in the festive green Guatemalan tablecloth draped around the foot of our Christmas tree was a gigantic dead rat displayed as tastefully as the gifts beside it.

Other thoughts keeping me awake are related to financial pressures, which are running high this month. Fortunately, these sorts of concerns do not block me up; to the contrary, they make me want to work harder, get the paintings out there, get the book in stores, make phone calls to book buyers, keep writing and painting. Creativity, it seems, is a spiritual-action answer to earthly problems. And when I get myself out of my own way, I become a clear and capable channel for practical solutions.

I am now guzzling chamomile tea in hopes of catching some sleep soon, but I have yet to come down from the ceiling. Skeleton Woman has cranked me up. I spent a good part of the day painting, then repainting horse bones and woman bones. Late in the afternoon, I caught a glimpse of the rider's face. She is laughing! And well she should be—she has survived the fire.

When I close my eyes I can picture her smile, and also tonight's ring around the moon. Brujo guarded me from the shadows while I gazed at the night sky for quite a long time this evening, admiring the shimmering ring. The moon will be full in a few days, bringing with it an eclipse, to be followed the next day by winter solstice. At that point the balance of dark and light will shift, changing the entire tone of our lives once again.

Christmas 1991

I'm enjoying the fading afternoon sun through my office window. In the golden light the cholla turns soft, as does the Spanish bayonet; each tiny spike is glistening and quivering in the breeze. Against a washed-out winter-blue sky, ominous clouds are wrapped around the peaks of the Catalinas.

Bob and I have been hiking in the afternoons while Sasha stays at home with a sitter, and we have just returned from a glorious trek. We trudged along the rugged Sutherland Trail for about three hours. After the first hour, we came upon a bed of huge boulders beneath a cascading stream. There on those rocks where the water talks I could feel the heartbeat of the earth. I have often set out on a hike in a state of despair, knowing God will overtake me on the trail.

Having accessed my spiritual source in the wilderness, I want to finish Skeleton Woman before the new year. Over the past few weeks, much of my creative energy has been siphoned off into shopping, but now the "inside boss" is saying, "Le Marque, get that painting done." For as long as I have been painting and writing, I have received instructions from this voice, and I have learned to get up and act on them.

The reason for taking immediate action is that particularly startling images often come to us at the crossroads of our lives and they must be painted quickly, before we lose sight of them forever. When such an image comes, if I don't pick up my brush or writing pad, my life is apt to change form so dramatically that the message may be irretrievably lost. Honoring these messages, as well as the body's desire to dance at inopportune moments, accelerates growth by activating interior forces. So it is that through creativity we grow in beauty and our radiance is magnified.

Tomorrow I plan to paint in a studio filled with women, including one or two who have not painted before. The new students will require considerable attention, yet I work best amid lots of distractions. I learned this about myself from an interesting psychic named George, whom I saw in Los Angeles years ago. Through the wreath of smoke that curled out of his pipe and into his brain, George told me that he saw me traveling around in something resembling a golden Gypsy wagon filled with all kinds of stuff. When I stopped and opened the door, "everything in the world spilled out." He saw me working best while in the midst of such a three-ring circus. Listening to him, I felt proud of the seeming chaos of my life, unaware that a few short months later I would be moving into my truck with everything I needed for living and painting. Though circumstances have shifted somewhat, I am still happy painting in the midst of a carnival.

A few minutes ago I was putting Sasha to sleep and succeeded in putting myself to sleep as well. As I drifted in and out of consciousness, images came to me of my mother lying dead. At first I was detached, simply remembering what she looked like with her upper lip elongated over her teeth. Then I saw myself coming into her room after learning that she had died. I rushed to her bed and climbed in next to her. Resting my face against hers, I nuzzled her for the last time and ran my warm hands over her cold hands and face. Tears were pouring from my eyes into the facial crevices left by seventy-four years of laughing and crying. She was simply beautiful and free at last, though I was devastated.

In the midst of these last intimate moments I was to have with my mother, I saw paramedics coming in the front door. My heart pounded in stark fear that they would somehow revive this woman who had been longing for death since the crossing over of my father a little more than two years before. One of the paramedics hooked up her equipment to

Mom's body. "I'm picking up a heartbeat!" she hollered to the others. I froze in horror, my fingers still touching my mother. "Take your hands off her," the paramedic ordered. "I need to get a reading." As sure as my heartbeat had once resounded through my mother's body, it was doing so again and registering as a "reading." That primal human connection had not been severed by the closing of the veil between worlds. It was time to take my hands off my mother.

After the wires and monitors were removed, I could not bring myself to touch her. In retrospect I could see that this intrusion into my final quiet moments with her was barbaric, but only because I was not prepared for the deathbed routine and was unable to think fast enough to tell the paramedic to leave me alone with my mom. Although the laws of Pima County required me to cut off the otherworldly flow of my long good-bye, I saw that no one could ever rob me of the beautiful way in which my mother chose to die—in her own time, in her own way, and with absolute clarity and focus.

Weeping beside the warm body of my sleeping daughter, I heard the familiar animal sounds of my grief breaking uncontrollably through the darkness. Roused from her deep sleep, Sasha stretched out an arm and wrapped it around my head. "Grandma and Grandpa are here looking after you," she whispered. "They won't let anything happen to you." Waking up more fully, she bolted upright and reached to the foot of the bed. In her hand was Gawky—a shredded, grayish, much loved scrap from one of my very worn cotton nightgowns, which has consoled her ever since the first night we left her with a baby-sitter. She ripped off a morsel of it and handed it to me thoughtfully, saying, "You need a Gawky, Mama."

She remained quiet for a few minutes, rubbing Gawky against her upper lip. "Not every people cry as much as you," she then said. "That's true, Sasha. Not many people do cry as much as I do, but they should. It makes the hurt feel better," I replied. "You and me are the only ones who cry this much," she added contemplatively. "That's because we're smart, honey bear. We're smart in the heart." She drifted off peacefully next to me, shoulder to shoulder, Gawky to Gawky.

December 26, 1991

I was able to work in depth on Skeleton Woman this morning. Holding the horse anatomy book in my left hand and a brush in my right, I painted while lying on the floor, climbing up the stepladder, then kneeling on the floor. When stiffness set in, I considered standing on my head, even swinging in circles from the ceiling fan.

Eventually, my students arrived. I was overjoyed to see them piling out of their cars with paint boxes, palettes, and glows of excitement. Jean Marie, who had not painted before, worked in watercolor; Margaret and Janee, who'd had a little experience painting, used oils for the first time. Whereas Jean Marie and Margaret set up shop in the studio, Janee worked outside on a painting of the beaver-tail cactus by the front door. While painting, we drank tea, listened to music, and didn't talk much. I always discourage chattering, telling my students: "Say hi, then get to work. We'll talk later. Put whatever you want to say, or the good feelings you have while being together, into your painting. Not talking forces the words into pictures."

As I alternated between spending time with Jean Marie and Margaret in the studio and Janee in the cold winter air under the mesquite tree, Bella—my dark-faced shadow dog—accompanied me. A good studio dog like Bella is a great asset to an artist. Such a companion can help you tolerate the loneliness that is often needed to do the work, either furnishing company or slinking quietly out of the way, depending on your mood. A sensitive studio dog will even know when to laugh at your jokes.

But mind you, a good studio dog does not require much in the way of entertainment. Your task is simply to ensure that all chicken bones and leftover Camembert are well out of reach and that the animal is properly fed and emptied. Your companion will then serve as an incentive to go for walks and ensure that you will never have to eat dinner alone. Because you're an artist—which by definition entitles you to a certain amount of eccentricity—you can even invite your dog to dine in a chair at the table with you.

Most importantly, a dog will not make inane comments about your art. Neither will a cat, for that matter. If you are an extremely sensitive type in search of a studio companion, a fish might be the way to go.

January 2, 1992

It's been seventeen years to the day since I've had a drink of alcohol. I'm astounded that I've stuck with sobriety for so long, but as a result of persevering I am immersed in a life that far surpasses my wildest dreams of decades ago. My creativity has flourished, and my days are filled with love and adventure. Seventeen years ago, on the other hand, all the love was dead and I had no hope, no future. This miraculous turn-about in my life awakens feelings of amazement and gratitude in me with each passing day.

These feelings persist despite a horrid experience I have just had with an art gallery—a visceral reminder of why I no longer do business with such operations. For two weeks I was trying to track down a large desert painting I've had on exhibit in California. The gallery, it appears, has closed, without notifying me and without bothering to return my painting. I've begun calling around to find out what became of the place, although I don't expect to ever see the painting again.

On a higher note, I spent New Year's Eve completing the painting of Skeleton Woman. It was a perfect way to usher in the new year. Executing this painting, which so genuinely depicts the initiation that unfolded after the death of my mother, was itself a rite of passage. Why? Because it has altered me on a cellular level, signaling a major growth spurt in my spiritual and emotional life. Working on Skeleton Woman has hurled me into the wall of burning grief and out the other side, liberated.

Now, with the death of my mother and the subsequent completion of this painting, my childhood is no longer smoldering, but charred. The pain of loss seared me to the bone; and the red paint that burned for days on the canvas became a *farolito* lighting the way for the return of my soul from passageways to the underworld. Aglow on the easel, it warmed my icy bones, stirring me back to life. Then as Skeleton Woman broke through the fire grinning and with a wreath of flowers on her head, I myself emerged as a new woman. I am burned clean of the fear of loss, the fear of dying, and the fear of watching loved ones walk through the doorway from this world to the next.

Chapter 6

Coyote Woman

Tucson, Arizona
January 6, 1992

When I took Sasha to preschool this morning, an insistent wind wrapped itself around us, whipping our hair and clothes tightly against our bodies. As we came onto the ridge leading down to River Road, we could see the advancing storm that was about to unleash itself on us. The angry clouds to the east had not yet closed their seam against the Rincon Mountains. The mountains, wrapped in mystery, were serenely blue, with a blanket of clouds dropping over their ridges and a luminous edge of white at the bottom of the dark folds. This radiant border, pumped with light from the sun rising just behind the clouds, shone like the hem on the robe of a goddess. It seemed like the right time to say our morning prayers.

My prayers resemble a phone conversation with a close friend that breaks off and resumes intermittently throughout the day. I don't say amen, because I never officially close down communication. In fact, at times I am tempted to substitute the word *furthermore.* This variation seemed apropos as the rain began to fall with a vengeance, leaving Sasha, who refuses to wear a jacket in winter, shivering hard.

In our driving-to-school prayer we asked to be shown what we are to learn today: "Please make sure we get the lessons. Show us where you want us to be, what you want us to do. Show us how we can be of service to you and your way of life. Help us be kind and have extra patience. Thank you for making sure we didn't fight this morning while getting ready to leave." We continued with thank yous for watering the mesquite trees, the palo verdes, the eucalyptus, and all the cactus plants. As we drove past a horse, we added a thank you for washing the horses. Then a samurai-type yell came bellowing out of my tiny blonde-haired child, who announced, "My new name is Princess Colleen Rose. And don't forget to turn off the rain when it's done." Sasha, who often concocts colorful names for herself, told me to yell this prayer "real loud," which we both did over and over again.

By the time I returned home, rain was pelting the earth. The road, fed by washes that crisscross the desert, was running thick and red. The seam of dense clouds between our house and the mountains all around us had been stitched up tight. Evidently, this storm is here for a while.

Having finished Skeleton Woman, I am experiencing a big letdown and little desire to work. Still, I am planning to stretch a four-by-six-foot canvas for Coyote Woman before our painting class on Thursday. I've been pulled to paint her since she first materialized, but she's been elusive and my life's been wiggly. In the meantime, she's become a part of my existence and I, no doubt, have become a part of hers. Now that there is a lull in the avalanche of my life, I may be able to coax her onto canvas.

Who is Coyote Woman? She is the utterly unpredictable and cosmically prankish, profoundly ruthless, sometimes vicious cause of all things orderly suddenly jumping out of place. When she's around, what was once reliable can no longer be counted on: the car battery gives out on your way to a job interview; the answering machine dies while you are waiting for an urgent call; the process server arrives in the middle of your workshop presentation at the same time a Federal Express delivery comes from the IRS and the period you so fervently prayed for begins leaking red on the back of your white dress as you sign for the package. Coyote Woman is why I don't have a white carpet—I just never know when she's going to pay a little surprise visit!

Surprise visits are customary here. Last Friday, for example, I had a sore back, and Bob was about to work on it in the backseat of the van before we went hiking. But I was suddenly overcome by gales of hysterical laughter for no apparent reason. For five minutes I lay on my stomach snorting and howling like a mad animal. Sometimes this entity takes over while I am speaking in public as well. On such occasions I either break out in laughter or fail to remember what I've just said.

At times, I am a coyote; it's something I've simply come to accept. At other times, I wake up and find I have become a rattlesnake. This shapeshifting is not something you can fight; you either learn to work with it or it hunts you down and eats you.

Following my unexpected "takeover" on Friday came a long unbalanced weekend. To begin with, I did not write. Sometimes the need to create has to build up again after you've completed a Big Painting. Exhibiting can have this effect, too, as can finishing a book.

Furthermore, I insisted on playing The Ultimate Mom all weekend and was defeated in part by my sore back. (Although I know it's time to stop lifting my kid, it's a hard devotion to give up.) When I told Sasha I needed to rest in bed, she went off to play by herself for hours—a new and much welcome pastime. I was glad to have discovered what I needed and to have communicated the information to her. It's an even greater pleasure to watch *her* discover *her* needs and find ways to meet them. As a four year old, she's a long way off from cooking dinner, unless I'm hungry for sand pies decorated with cactus spines and dead beetles. Nonetheless, we had two solid "girls days," which pleased her no end.

I generate energy, use it, build it up, store it, and explode with it; then I must be a blob for a while. That's the creative cycle. Catch the waves while they're high, for the tide will soon roll out.

January 7, 1992

While driving down River Road this morning, after delivering the kid to school, I began to realize why I create six-foot, eight-foot, and twelve-foot paintings. The reason is that these are not only paintings of dancers but also the canvases on which they dance. The room fills with an electrical charge when these figures emerge, choose their rattles and drums, and paint their faces using my hands. The paintings are large because they are *alive!*

January 10, 1992

Yesterday's painting class got me thinking about how well teaching works for me, especially when self-directed students dream up their own projects and I help bring them out. There were four students—Janee, Jean Marie, Margaret, and Frances, who paints like a criminal defense attorney. As we were sailing along, painting and drinking tea, Janee piped up with, "I feel like throwing something." In response I took her hand, and we went out into the desert. There we found rocks and threw them; we also found pieces of wood and saguaro ribs, which we beat on the ground while yelling. Our best find was a rolled-up piece of chicken wire about the size of a small person. After shaping it into a human figure, I beat it with my saguaro-rib club. Janee, for her part, had come upon a piece of black wire that she used as a whip. When we returned to the studio, we were outside of ourselves; emotionally cleansed, we painted like fiends.

After class I flashed onto the endless nighttime litany of questions I churned with years ago as a first-time teacher: What if it rains? What if I can't think of anything to say? What if I look scared? What if I sweat, stutter, can't find the right words? What if I'm frightened of my students, or of my own shadow? Months passed before it dawned on me that what most sets students at ease is a teacher's *humanity* and *willingness to be real.* To move beyond comfort and make magic, you need, in addition to creative students, a *pregathering ritual* to slow you down and an *ability to "see" and "hear" with your heart.*

Before class begins, I slow myself down. I put on music and decide what we're going to listen to as a group—classical first, then rhythms and melodies conducive to diving into the self. I make a giant pot of tea and set out beautiful Japanese cups. Then I open the windows to let the desert in, and I get quiet.

During class, I work alongside the students, making sure to "show up" inside my body. I look and listen with the heart, and encourage them to do the same by getting their "noses out of their paintings." This we do by setting our easels a good distance away and taking time to examine the canvases. The purpose of this exercise, I tell my students, is never to trash a painting but rather to methodically pick out, one by one, areas that need more work. After correcting these spots, we put the pieces up again, repeating the process until we are happy with the results.

I also encourage my students to identify what they need in order to make the improvements. Some, like Janee in yesterday's class, want to go into the desert and throw rocks; other need to curl up into a little ball and have a good cry; still others need to write. Many possibilities exist for the action that must occur before anything else can take place.

January 13, 1992

It's nearly 9:00 P.M. Sasha is tucked in my bed, pizza is in the oven, and as it warms, my mind turns to thoughts of Coyote Woman. She is a trickster with a mean streak in her. When all is well, she likes to come and throw a wrench into the works. Although it's often exactly what is needed, she is merciless. In painting her I leave myself open to her tricks.

Interacting with any of the archetypes is dangerous, for while they can be formidable allies, they can also be horrendous nightmares. Coyote Woman, for her part, has a way of exploding seemingly stable lives and blowing belief systems to smithereens. It was after she trotted unseen through my life in Los Angeles that an important relationship dissolved and I wound up living in my truck.

Earlier this evening I was thinking back to when I first began to identify myself as an artist, and soon afterward, as a writer too. It was a big deal to stand up straight and say, "My name is Tina. I'm an artist and a writer." Claiming my true identity as a creative person who does not fit in the usual world, or play by rules that work for the majority of the population, inspired me to make my own place in the world and discover my own rules. After shedding various false identities and admitting to my real job, I became a much stronger version of the woman I was in my twenties and thirties.

I spent hours today wandering from shop to shop hunting for the darkest purple velvet. While rummaging through turquoise beads and sterling buttons, I was in pack-rat heaven. I never did find the shade of velvet that sparked this quest, but it did not matter, for my pleasure was in the hunt, in the luxury I had of following any impulse about where to go or what to poke into. Searching through bead and fabric shops, I touched each item that called to me, leaving no stone unturned. Stepping into an office supply store, I indulged a whim to buy a box of expensive paper. Crossing the parking lot, I sat in a Japanese restaurant and wrote for nearly an hour. It was a day of getting enough—a great stealing-time treat for any woman with a family.

I felt like I was having an affair with myself! This sort of activity is desperately needed after the death of a family member or dear friend. When people we deeply love die, parts of us die with them and other parts have to be dragged back from the abyss.

January 16, 1992

Last night I visited Namka. Speaking softly, she walked me through the doorway to the other world. There I came upon the body of a woman who resembled me. She was lying belly-down on the earth, and ten swords were sticking out of her back.

A second woman emerged from the underbrush of a dense forest. In slow motion she pulled the swords out of the prone woman's back and, gathering them in her arms, carried them deep into the forest to her cottage. There she planted them in the garden. Soon strange and beautiful flowers began to grow from them. The flowers were bell-shaped and huge, up to three feet in diameter.

Turning, I saw a heart suspended in midair over the garden. It had been pierced by three swords aimed at the earth. An unseen force pushed the swords downward till they clattered to the ground. Out of the three wounds in the heart came a tiny rattlesnake, a coyote, and a mourning dove all speaking in tinny voices.

At this point I felt Namka's hand at my back, then a shove, followed by the strange sensation of being skewered. Still in a trance, I saw a number of swords going into my back and pushing out through my chest. With that, I experienced a surge of freed energy.

An unseen being then placed something round in my hands. Looking down, I saw a six-inch bowl made of highly reflective metal. After cupping the bowl to the area between and slightly above my eyes, I moved it slowly down my body, then placed it upright on top of my head.

Returning to consciousness, I noticed the waxing moonlight on the desert. Now, twenty-four hours later, I am intrigued by these images.

On the easel is a four-by-six-foot canvas waiting for Coyote Woman. I have opened my little black drawing book to the page where I first drew her last February, when she came dancing out of the twilight shouting, "Hey, hey, hey," the shadows fleeing before her. She wants to come out of the formless world where I see her dancing. I wonder if her appearance in my studio will bring disaster or if she is merely a harbinger of change.

January 17, 1992

It's 5:00 A.M. and about five days short of a full moon. After considerable squirming and howling on the part of Sasha, whom we cannot seem to keep out of our bed, I found that I was unable to sleep. Rarely can I sleep during this phase of the moon.

A memory has just come to me. Several months ago, right after my mother died, Namka invited me to her office. I was glad to go, for I had been troubled by great fears about growing older. I trusted her to hold the doorway open for me to slip over to the other side.

Once there, I saw a beautiful dark-haired woman who was one of my ancestors. I asked for her name. "That's not important," she replied. "Go out into the desert and sit on the bare earth. While seated, feel the heartbeat and warmth of your mother, the earth. You need to do this often." She showed me what appeared to be a piece of iridescent fabric revealing an undulating plane of shapes that at first looked like large fish scales. Gazing more intently, I saw they were outlines of women's faces.

"These are the women in your clan who have come before you," the dark-haired woman explained. "Look at the river of beauty they create. You are a part of this living fabric of women, so do not waste one more precious moment of your life worrying about the physical changes that come with aging. Real beauty—beauty of the spirit—is timeless. Your true beauty is not influenced by your exterior appearance. You are a radiant woman."

Speechless, I watched the flowing river of women whose blood runs through my body. As their movements pulsed, I felt an answering beat throughout my being. And ever since I became privy to the collective knowledge emanating from this tapestry of women, I have been far less plagued by fears about growing older. Now when I'm wondering, is that a gray hair? I tell myself, "No, it's silver and very valuable."

Yesterday Janee, whose funds have run low, and I finalized negotiations on a trade of art lessons for a quilt she's working on. The colors of the quilt are purple, turquoise, paisley, and deep red on a black field; the stitches, small and precise. As she laid out this treasure on the kitchen table, I knew it would be magnificent on the lodge-pole bed I sleep in.

Although there is an art to working out arrangements of this sort, the payoff is tremendous. In this instance, I will be sleeping under Janee's quilt for many years to come and I will continue to enjoy her presence in painting class. Actually, her companionship has been invaluable to me ever since I arrived in Tucson. She is a woman of formidable intellect who's fun to dance with on the mental plane. What's more, she notices and acknowledges her feelings; her inner journey is intricate and demanding; and although she thinks she is "broken," she is a relentless seeker of healing.

Last week Janee took me on one of her favorite hikes at Saguaro National Monument. The sky was sunny and the air crisp as we headed up a steep trail to a stone fortress. There, after looking out at the expanse of land and sky, we dove into the cookies and tangerines she had brought, and broke out bottles of water. Soon the air turned biting, at which point we took shelter behind a sun-warmed stone, where we swapped morsels of our history in the way that women do, alternately laughing and crying. As the wind became more piercing, we huddled close to each other, and Janee, taking out a book, began to read aloud the poetry of Raymond Carver. His images of feelings and death drove me to crying. "Hold me," I pleaded. Janee held me and read while we both wept. For an hour and a half we stayed there like two desert lizards, soaking in the sun and watering the boulders with our tears. Then we headed back to the car cackling like jays and making our own rich little quilt of closeness. Such is the beauty of women's friendships.

Today in painting class, I worked on Coyote Woman and she worked on me. She danced out onto the canvas waving her dancing stick and yip-yapping. I was both surprised and not surprised by her level of cooperation. During painting class I was able to spend a few minutes getting her lightly sketched in oil. "She wants a hot, hot pink, and so she shall have it," I told myself. This burning pink is a powerful color, though not one I often work with.

After a while I noticed tears streaming down Jean Marie's face, whereupon we retired to the couch for a good cry. She is being called by one of those mysterious inner voices to go to Los Angeles, she indicated. My compassion was immediately aroused, for I'm aware that not many people are tuned into this station and that those who are work for a very demanding "employer." Despite the desire to follow our inner guidance, we feel a terrible loneliness and strangeness about it all. "Why can't I live an ordinary life?" we ask. "Why can't I keep the same job, house, and husband?" The truth is that there's no way we can.

I feel a great kinship with Jean Marie even though I have only known her a few months. How much I will miss her couldn't be stated without honoring the learning experiences and adventures she is meant to have. "It is the City of the Angels you're going to," I reminded her. "There will always be a place for you in my studio and in my heart."

January 18, 1992

I am writing this entry while driving. With each left turn, my writing pad goes round and round on the steering wheel, but no feeling must go uncaptured. Why record all these emotions? So I can read them during the next painful cycles of learning and change; remember the way back if I lose myself; call up pictures of people I have loved and who have loved me; recall the lightning strikes that radically change my life; and never forget that I can flourish no matter what.

We have decided to stay in Tucson, at least for a while. Although stability does not provide the delicious agony that inspires some of my most transformative works of art, I'm accomplishing a great deal more than I was while living in my truck. As my friend Jeanne said after I voiced amazement about the amount of work coming out, "It's like the dam broke."

At this point I am writing while walking through a department store. There's too much stirring inside me to put down my pad. Invaded by an itch that can only be relieved by making something, I write and walk and live.

January 30, 1992

At 8:00 A.M. I plunked the kid in the bathtub, as she requested, and raced down the hall to record my notes from yesterday. Stepping into my office, I noticed that the dogs had eaten a yellow sponge with a green "scrubby" on one side, for there it was barfed up on the carpet! And there it stayed while I did my writing, trying not to look at the goo on the floor except when the dogs attempted to steal it and re-eat it.

Now I am guarding my breakfast from them. Although I've had only a few bites of a doctored-up bagel, I have managed to smear salmon and cream cheese around my hand and up my arm. I refuse to spend this minuscule scrap of writing time cleaning up anything—neither my left hand nor dog barf. For me, writing is about jumping off a cliff and flowing with a fast-running stream. It's about coming back to life, running back to life. Sasha will be howling for attention soon enough, at which point writing time will be over.

February 4, 1992

Most people, I've noticed, resist surrendering to creative urges. Some resist because they fear there is no creativity in them, or no talent for expressing it; others fear they will be consumed by a swiftly moving stream of creative impulses. Yet what happens if we give creativity a shot only to find that one painting is all that's in there? And what if that measly little painting stinks? At the very least, we may discover that it is better to paint than not to paint, or that one image must be birthed to make way for the next. If we give in completely, on the other hand, what will become of us? Will our creativity demand that we give our entire life to it? Probably so—but it will be a life worth living, an enviable life. The choice is ours: we can opt for total surrender or lifelong regret.

Dealing with my own creativity has been similar to dealing with my dreams. The more attentively I listen, the more often the "magical maiden" appears. The more I honor this process by validating the images that arise, the more meaningful they become. I prepare my workplace and leave it set up. I keep a writing pad in my car. I draw and write on place mats, the backs of envelopes, anything within reach. I get up and work in the middle of the night, because that is often the only time I've got. Always, I record the images and words that come, no matter how strange or disturbing they may be.

As a result of these mad practices, what was once a stream has become a river. And instead of losing myself, I have found myself—hidden in a deep green canyon by a spring. At first I observed an infinite waterfall, stunning to behold. Far more beautiful, however, was the woman standing beneath it naked and shimmering. In merging with the waters of the river I have come into my own power. I have become the woman I always wanted to be, a person I would never have known had I not started out on this blind journey.

Because of cultural taboos that prevail against living a wonderful life, it's hard for creative people to let themselves put on their wings. Many are held back by unspoken peer pressure, if not outright hostility: "How dare you be so free, so irresponsible. Get back up here on the conveyor belt." Having stepped off the conveyor belt, I often feel the crowd watching breathlessly behind me, wondering, "What will happen to her? Will she get back in line?" Half the watchers want to see me fall on my face; the others want to see the wings sprout out and the woman flying. This fifty-fifty opinion split characterizes not only the crowd but also each person in it, including artists themselves. If I stay my course, a lot of people are going to make a run for the sparkly box marked "Wings."

Chapter 7

The Fork in the Road

Tucson, Arizona
February 6, 1992

The day before yesterday I felt as if I had the flu and yet I didn't really think I was sick. With absolute conviction I explained to two people that my dad had just died, only to realize that it was my mom who recently died. Then around 4:00 P.M. Dave Hoobler, who puts on our workshops in Mazatlán, said, "It's the anniversary of your father's death. I saw it in your book. Could *this* have anything to do with how you're feeling?" Hearing that, I cried for a half hour, lonely for my crazy old family.

Now I am lonely again. It's 11:00 P.M. and few minutes ago I was disturbed by a chorus of coyotes, followed by dead silence—a desert opera that does not bode well for Puma, who has been outdoors for hours. I hope this coyote song did not signify the end of our miniature black panther who loves to fill the yard with headless gifts. Only yesterday, intestines were strewn about like discarded carnival streamers; counting the unattached feet, livers, noses, and tails, I estimated a total of two mice.

Like a proper wild mother, I have spent many nights fretting over this heartless hunter. Then just before dawn, in he'd stagger quite full of himself, and I'd fawn over his lithe black body. Right now, the desert is so quiet that I can't imagine how I'll fall asleep.

In spite of myself I went back to sleep. I dreamed I was in my old family home evicting various people who had come for the weekend and moved in. Some were dressed in Grecian gowns, and others in Egyptian regalia; a few sported gold wings. First, I threw out my aunt. Setting her flat on the floor, I placed my hands on her face and proceeded to hypnotize her, saying, "You will be out by Monday." Next, I took a relative's husband by the lapels and said, "Out by Monday. I want to make sure you understand that—out by Monday." I worried that I was giving them too much time, that they might steal things.

I am immersed in a period of major housecleaning and am calling in my allies to roust out what I cannot reach or should not touch. The people and things that belong with me will remain; those that no longer fit must be shoved out.

As I return to my own life, I am surprised by the radical change in Bob. For weeks he was so cold and distant that I was preparing myself for the proverbial "fork in the road." I did not beg or pull at him in any way; I simply commended myself into the care of God and jumped, all the while praying and talking. Sometimes the talking was mixed with smoldering. "Here's how I feel," I'd say. "What's going on with you?" His uncustomary refusal to talk told me we were on the edge of our relationship. My insides were screaming to him, "Come back and be in your body. Come back before I leave."

God has never kept me for long with a person who isn't with me in spirit one hundred percent. When the man I am with ceases to honor me, God removes me, often violently and suddenly. Leaving isn't something I get to vote on, which is a terrifying situation. This time, however, I was not removed. Ultimately, Bob and I did reach the dreaded fork, and as of now we are moving in the same direction.

Some of the strain we are under has come from all the death and loss of the last three years, combined with the intense and extremely stressful caregiving of my mother. As the splinters of emotional glass work their way to the surface, they cut at the heart again and again. Anger we have had to suppress forces its way out, and its painful emergence often turns us against each other. How do people survive such devastating losses strung together like successive torpedo hits? How do *couples* endure?

During the ordeal of the last few years, I was openly angry with my mother. We fought frequently, and I was often bitchy. I also expressed this anger verbally in support groups, freely venting my frustrations to women friends. I suppose that's why I'm faring better than I have since my dad's death.

Bob, on the other hand, was wonderful with my mother. His patience seemed limitless; swallowing his anger, he did the right thing by her. But I think it nearly broke him. In what I can only guess was a delayed reaction, he moved into a cold and distant rage, eventually leaving his body. Now he is back, though everything feels uncertain. Puma, it appears, has also returned from *his* romp on the wild side, and now I can relax a bit.

February 9, 1992

Although I love all the activity, the interesting people, and the wild and magnificent desert here in Tucson, I draw strength in knowing that one day I'll be going home to Santa Fe. Any time I become frightened at the prospect of the future, I tell myself I'll be okay once I return to the place where lilacs bloom against adobe walls.

I think of New Mexico like I used to think of my parents when they were in this world. No matter what happened, no matter how bad or scary my predicament was, I could go to them and sleep safely in the bed they always had ready. They were my refuge.

February 12, 1992

While waiting for my morning tea to steep, I am watching a pair of woodpeckers whack away at the huge palo verde tree in front of the house. I have opened the window a crack to hear them. The interior of the house, too, is alive with morning sounds: Sasha is getting ready for school and Bob is loudly searching for his glasses. This commotion may well turn into a come-in-here-and-take-over decree. First, though, there is breakfast to be made, and a school lunch as well.

I woke up thinking about my special times with Sasha. Every night, we go out into the desert to sit in the hot tub. Once suitably boiled, we wrap up in giant Turkish towels, she lies back in my arms, and we stargaze. I often end up looking at her sweet face lifted skyward, her straw-colored hair pale in the darkness as she scans the heavens for the "sparkliest" stars.

Several nights ago, when Bob was out of town, Sasha and I had a candlelight dinner. We made minestrone soup with pesto and a salad of oak leaf lettuce and arugula from our garden. She sat on my lap for most of the meal, then suddenly she leaned back as big pools of tears collected in the corners of her eyes. We cried together, missing Didi—Sasha's pet name for my mother. "She was your mommy, Didi?" my little one asked. "Yes, and I miss my mommy," I told her. "She was my Didi," Sasha replied, "and she's never coming back."

After about ten minutes of holding and hugging, Sasha asked to have her arms tickled. I recognized this as a request for the agonizing, tantalizing tickle designed to hypnotize rather than evoke laughter. Artfully, I tickled her, and soon her arms were covered with tiny goose bumps. Right away, she filled the room with a laughter that lifted my spirits and brought a smile. In the midst of our sadness, life beamed out its radiance.

It's now later in the morning, and I've gone to great lengths to secure this quarter hour to write. Like a creature with eight arms, I flung breakfast on the table, did an impression of a python with a bagel, and concocted the usual kid lunch of vegetarian gourmet tidbits—though I never know if these delicacies get eaten or fed to the class gerbil. After that, I had a knock-down fight with Bob over our anxiety-provoking finances and, tinged with an adrenaline glow, rushed back to my desk.

Sasha, absorbed in a before-school movie on the tube, looked up at me and, aware that I would tell her to entertain herself until the timer went off fifteen minutes later, lassoed Bob. I'm trying to resist the automatic mother-mechanism that has me perennially getting up to take care of the child. "She'll be fine if I don't run into the playroom as Supermom," I tell myself. My daughter is never going to learn to put herself first in life if I don't show her how it's done.

February 15, 1992

One of the great gifts of Tucson is its women. My first friend here was Heidi, the real estate agent who found this house for us. Heidi grew up in Tucson and knows the city like the back of her hand. Her support during my mom's death was unbeatable: she got me out of the house—once, as far as Nogales, Mexico—she got me crying, and she somehow got me laughing.

Tucson is a magnet for strong women such as Heidi. I have availed myself of their offerings, and they have restored me.

February 23, 1992

This past week I have been too preoccupied to write. My days and nights have been filled with a constant stream of pressing business concerns, legal matters, and other left-brain dilemmas that demand my attention. Whenever possible, I've also surrendered to the intoxicating effects of spring.

The writing I now do is on small notes scribbled in hard-to-read scrawl in my car at red lights, or while waiting in garages, or between catastrophes the devil-dogs dream up. I spend a good deal of what used to pass for free time repairing the house after the dogs careen through it on their kamikaze raids, and picking up after them in what would otherwise be a beautiful garden. Invariably, the dog leavings come out with shreds of our clothing either braided through them or wrapped around them. At Christmas time everything came out woven with tinsel and ribbon. The good news is that this weft seems to clear up their diarrhea.

I am working on a painting of a little cross I originally drew on a cocktail napkin; it is adorned with a blazing sun, and decorating the border are small moons, stars, more suns, and Saturn. This image reminds me of Santa Fe, where enigmatic crosses jut out from the red dirt in isolated places. After spending so many years as a non-Catholic kid in a Catholic school, I guess I'm finally making peace with the image, at least artistically.

March 3, 1992

It's nearly 6:00 A.M. and I've been awake for about three hours, trying to read, meditate, and trance. But nothing is flowing—probably because I am wired with stage fright over a speaking engagement coming up in Walnut Creek, California, later this week. In a recurring waking dream I've been having, fifteen people show up to hear me speak at an auditorium that seats two hundred, and I am filled with dread at my incompetence. Then I step up to speak and can't think of a thing to say.

No matter how often I speak in public—which is already far more than I was designed for—or how well the previous talk has gone, I enter an anticipatory state of near cardiac arrest. One of these days I may disintegrate from fear and, having dissolved, let the talk come through.

This trip to California will be one of my few excursions away from the homestead since Sasha was born. Although I'll be gone only one night, I'll use my time alone to dive deep inside. Over the years, I have learned to savor all moments of solitude.

My bag is packed with totems: sage and other desert plants, several writing pads, my rock collection, and pictures of my family. Tomorrow I'll toss in tapes for chanting and dancing, my black drawing book and brush pen, as well as Webster the Penguin, the stuffed animal I currently sleep with—all of which will fit quite well in my little suitcase with wheels. Traveling in my cowgirl boots and pulling my suitcase, I'll be able to go on foot for miles if I have to.

In addition to planning my gear and travel apparel, I am wondering who will show up and why. I am most curious to see which part of *me* will show up. Surely, it will be a new and improved version, and I'm looking forward to meeting her.

As I lie here in my office, which presently feels more like a cave, the windows are wide open to the early morning air and I am wrapped in my robe and a warm blanket, with my dogs beside me. It is as though I am in the desert, a woman with her wild dogs out under the open sky. The faintest light is filtering through the purple sky, yet no images are coming to be painted. I feel strange, cut off, not quite myself, as I often do when I am changing personalities.

March 6, 1992

I'm in the airplane with my seat belt fastened, about to take off for Walnut Creek to present a talk on creativity, followed the next day by a workshop for women, and my first book signing as well. Having arrived with plenty of time for a leisurely check-in, I wandered through the terminal, where I spotted a woman working at a shoe-shine stand that was nothing short of a tiny palace. Three steps led up to two thrones graced with little footrests.

Up I climbed—something I'd never before been drawn to do, but here I was on my way to an adventure. As the woman began working on my elegant elk cowgirl boots, I became flooded with memories of my father, who had looked after my boots ever since I received my first good pair from Hermes in Paris. Each time I visited my parents while in my twenties and thirties, Dad would step over to the carved wooden bench where he kept his polishes and soft brushes. "Take off your boots," he would say, eyeing the leather and proceeding to tell me just how to care for it. Slipping one hand inside a boot, he would use the other to brush off the dust and lather up the surface with saddle soap. As he cleaned and conditioned my boots, we would talk about my boyfriends and paintings. Always, he used the best polish—it went on smooth and rich, like lithography ink—and finished the job with a big, soft shoe-shine brush, which I've since inherited.

I often found it touching that this brilliant man who was nominated for three Academy Awards and who edited some of the most influential films of the century was using his talented hands to shine my boots. This, however, was only one of our father-daughter rituals. Dad and I would also lunch at his studio from time to time, take duck-hunting trips to Oregon, or go shooting with his retrievers. Odd little reprieves were common, for we were an odd little family.

Bringing myself back from this wave of memories, I gazed at the interesting woman shining my boots. "My name is Kathy," she said, adding that she owns the business herself, including the beautiful wooden stand I was on as well as a second stand in another terminal. A serious businesswoman, she works three days a week and takes calls between shifts from the pay phone across the walkway.

She's not only her own boss, I concluded, but also an artist in shoe care, carrying on the old tradition for lovers of fine leathers. Watching her carefully, I saw that she knew all the tricks. She lathered the saddle soap just so to get the desert dust out of the minute crevices in the leather. "Always clean that dust out of the cracks before you polish," she instructed me. "Use water to make the saddle soap foam," she explained while deftly applying clear nail polish to the small nicks in the surface of my boots.

I asked her about her life, and she asked me about mine. "How long have you been doing this?" I queried. "Forever—thirteen years," she replied. "It's fun."

"What brought you to Tucson?" she asked. "Came here with my mother, to take care of her. She was dying." "Did she die?" Kathy wanted to know. "Yes, in September." "They're not supposed to do that," she commented sorrowfully.

Kathy was accessible, interested in everything I had to say, and even curious about the title of my book. "*I*'m a warrior woman," she declared when I told her. "I could see that from across the terminal," I replied. "You've made your own life."

When Kathy finished attending to my boots, I asked what her services cost. "Three bucks," she said. And well worth it, I thought to myself, not only for the care you took but for the opportunity I had to spend a few moments with a woman warrior—a woman who holds the reins of her own horse.

Chapter 8

Crow Mother Comes Dancing Slowly

Tucson, Arizona
March 18, 1992

I've just returned from a night of dreaming. In one dream I was visiting people in a condominium complex when suddenly I heard a warning: "The sand is beginning to blow!" I ducked into my small cottage, even though the center of the ceiling was open to the sky. Automatically, a transparent roof began to slide across the opening, and as it did I could see piles of deadly sand billowing across the narrowing slit that remained. "Thank God my friends and I are inside," I told myself.

I could also see mounds of sand piling up against the sides of buildings, and small drifts accumulating in nearby cottages. Then the sandstorm ended as unpredictably as it had started. I was unnerved by the sight of great mounds of sand heaped on top of the mountains surrounding us, and the sky amber with small dust particles. The swimming pool, too, was sand covered, with several inches of grit on its steps and up to about three feet in other places.

At this point, I woke up anxious and unable to go back to sleep. There was something foreboding about the catastrophic storm. The sands are shifting again, I thought. Something is about to change, and I am filled with dread. Recording the dream helped dispel the fear.

In the morning I awakened from another dream of a deadly sandstorm. This time I reached for Sasha, wrapping my arms around her to reassure myself that she was really with me. The dream began in a photography store operated by actor Mel Gibson. Bella, the dark German shepherd, was with me, and a few people were ahead of us in line. My plan was to ask Mel if I could rent a new video camera, although my real intention was to tell him I had a terrible crush on him and wanted to sleep with him.

Suddenly, I saw a small blonde femme fatale whispering to him. Why would he want to sleep with me, I wondered, if he's involved with this type of woman? She was living with him, it turned out, and the three of us decided to take Bella for a walk. Although I was disgusted to be seen with her, I figured there must have been something I was supposed to do in this situation. But as we walked onto a beach, Mel vaporized. The woman did, too.

Before long, I saw Bob sitting on the tailgate of a Japanese hatchback parked in the sand. The wind was at our backs, coming off the sea. Registering a strong danger signal as the hair prickled on the back of my neck, I turned to see quickly shifting sands and wind coming up like a tornado. I scrambled to pick up our things, grabbed our shoes and car keys, and ran, for I knew a tidal wave was coming.

A few yards to my right I saw Sasha standing naked in the sand. "Quick, honey bear, get dressed," I told her as I frantically threw armfuls of clothes and boots in the back of the car. "Run, honey—quick like a bunny! Run ahead of me. I'll catch up with you and Daddy."

As Sasha dashed into the blowing sand, I jumped into the front seat of the car and fumbled for the key. Finding it at last, I spotted Sasha running about thirty feet ahead, started the car, but forgot to pull the door shut.

I woke up filled with anxiety and relieved to find my daughter asleep with her head on my shoulder. Closing my eyes again, I saw myself driving beside her, calling to her as I reached out and scooped her into my arms. Driving faster, I caught up with Bob, who leaped into the passenger seat. I floored the car, attempting to get us as far away from the coast as possible before the big wave hit.

This dream, too, has left me anxious. Waves and sandstorms, I know, foreshadow change.

How curious it is that in the six months since my mother died I have hardly remembered a dream and now I am able to recall two in a row! I wonder why my dreams have not been reaching me from the underworld. Ever since I was little, my mother and I would tell each other our dreams, marveling at the images and strange events. I suppose that mysterious flowering garden is still there, buried under a mountain of grief.

March 19, 1992

Two new students are coming to the Thursday morning workshop. One is Patti, an expressive woman who's been through a lot of therapy and whom I know from the women's group. When I asked her if she would like to come paint with us, she was surprised. "I've never done artwork. I wouldn't even know how to start," she said. "That's not your problem," I told her. "It's mine. You're always waving your hands around in the air. Just let me put some paint-filled brushes in them and the colors will fly out."

I initially approached Patti about joining our group because she's planning to move to New Zealand later this year, and I thought she would want to take the workshop experience with her, as something she could turn to for the rest of her life. Then I remembered that with her entire top layer collapsing as it is, painting would give her a tool for diving inside to salvage the parts that warrant saving. I also figured she would be an ideal student, because she's open-minded, able to follow directions, and instinctively adept at putting color to her moods. I am sure this will be a good send-off; after all, it's easy to forget the people you've worked with and even those you've slept with, but you never forget the people you've painted with.

The second new student coming this week is Jane, whom I know from meetings we've both attended. Over the past few weeks I have seen her transform from a people-pleaser into a weeping, melting woman. The pain of becoming real is as intense as the pain of labor, though harder to recognize as a gift. So when Jane asked to join us, I was delighted.

In addition to Patti and Jane, the workshop circle will include Janee, whose feelings and dreams now move fluidly onto canvas, and Frances, who laughs with pleasure while painting. Together, they'll be an unusually harmonious group of women. In the courtyard on the other side of the French doors all kinds of spring flowers will be blooming—which is what *we'll* be doing indoors.

March 21, 1992

To celebrate the equinox, I went to see ancient rock art with a local archaeological group. Everywhere, the desert was lush with wildflowers. At Signal Hill, in Saguaro National Monument, the petroglyphs were beautiful and clear. A sluggish young rattler lay coiled, sunning itself on the rocks piled near a series of spirals pecked into the desert patina. We were unafraid, since it was too cold and too early in the season for a snake to be dangerous.

At Picture Rocks, in the northwestern part of Tucson, I became absorbed in pictographs of bighorn sheep, turtles, and tiny humans. I was sure that long ago I, too, had carved images in stone and rubbed earthen colors into the scratches.

I have planted hundreds of seeds in our garden. Sometimes Sasha joins me, with her hole-making stick and a handful of seed packets. Last night, just before the equinox, she was having a hard time falling asleep, so I helped her slip into her pink moccasins with sparkles. Then we went out to the courtyard and planted our remaining seeds by moonlight.

Over the past few days we planted sunflowers galore, cosmos, marigolds, and zinnias. We put out zucchini and yellow crookneck squash. Then we filled whatever space was left with arugula and oak leaf lettuce, which we consume like wild horses.

I am coming back to life after the death of my parents. I cannot seem to plant enough seeds and flowers. Most days, my hands are deep in the mud, assisting in the ceremonial rebirth of the earth, my family, and myself.

March 23, 1992

This evening Puma, while accompanying us on an evening walk far out of his territory, disappeared once again. By bedtime I was restless and worried about him, so I got dressed and walked the surrounding washes in the darkness. There I pleaded with him to come home and sent silent warnings that Puma, being only a hole where a cat used to be, would be bad juju for a coyote to eat.

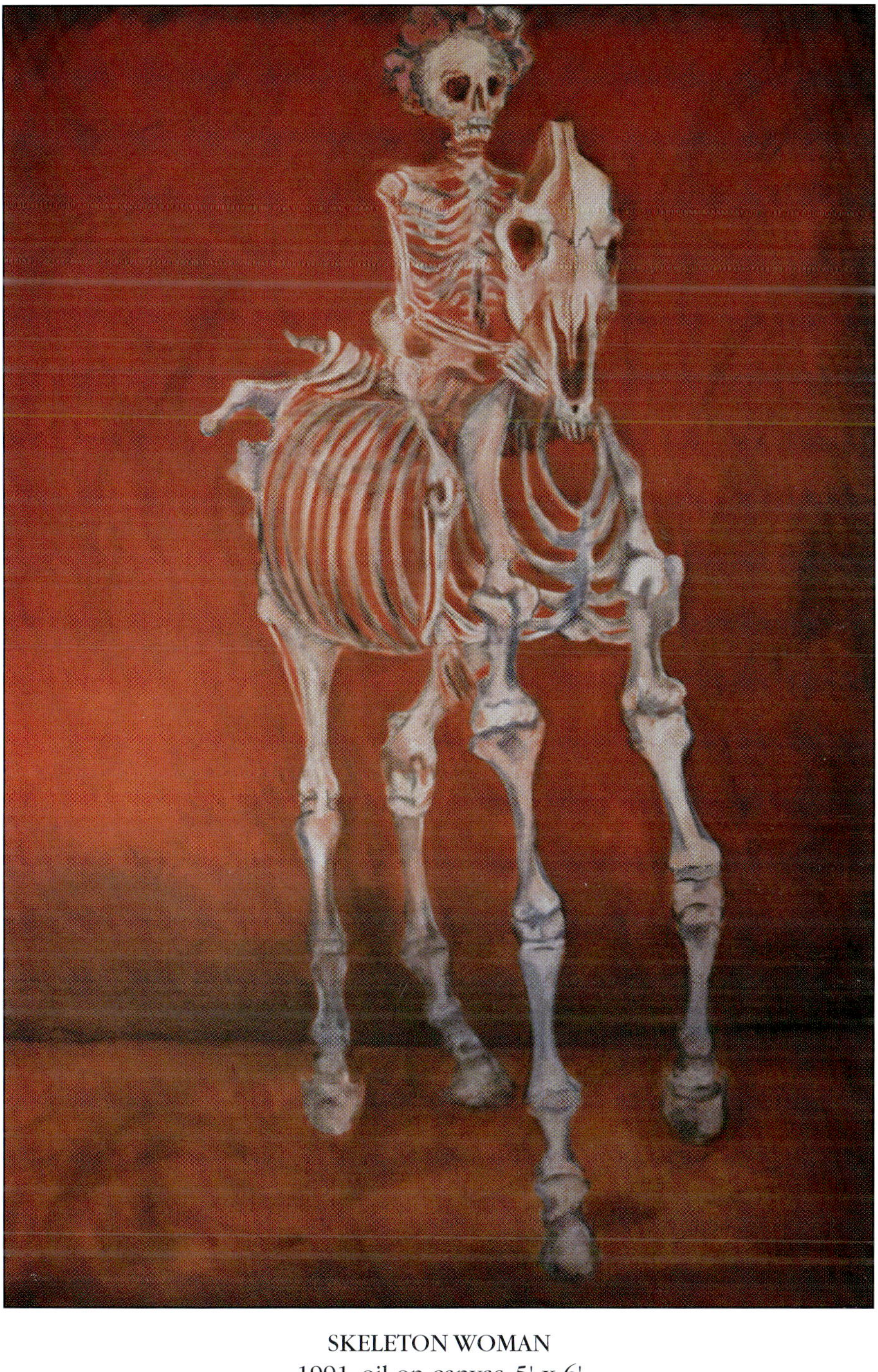

SKELETON WOMAN
1991, oil on canvas, 5' x 6'

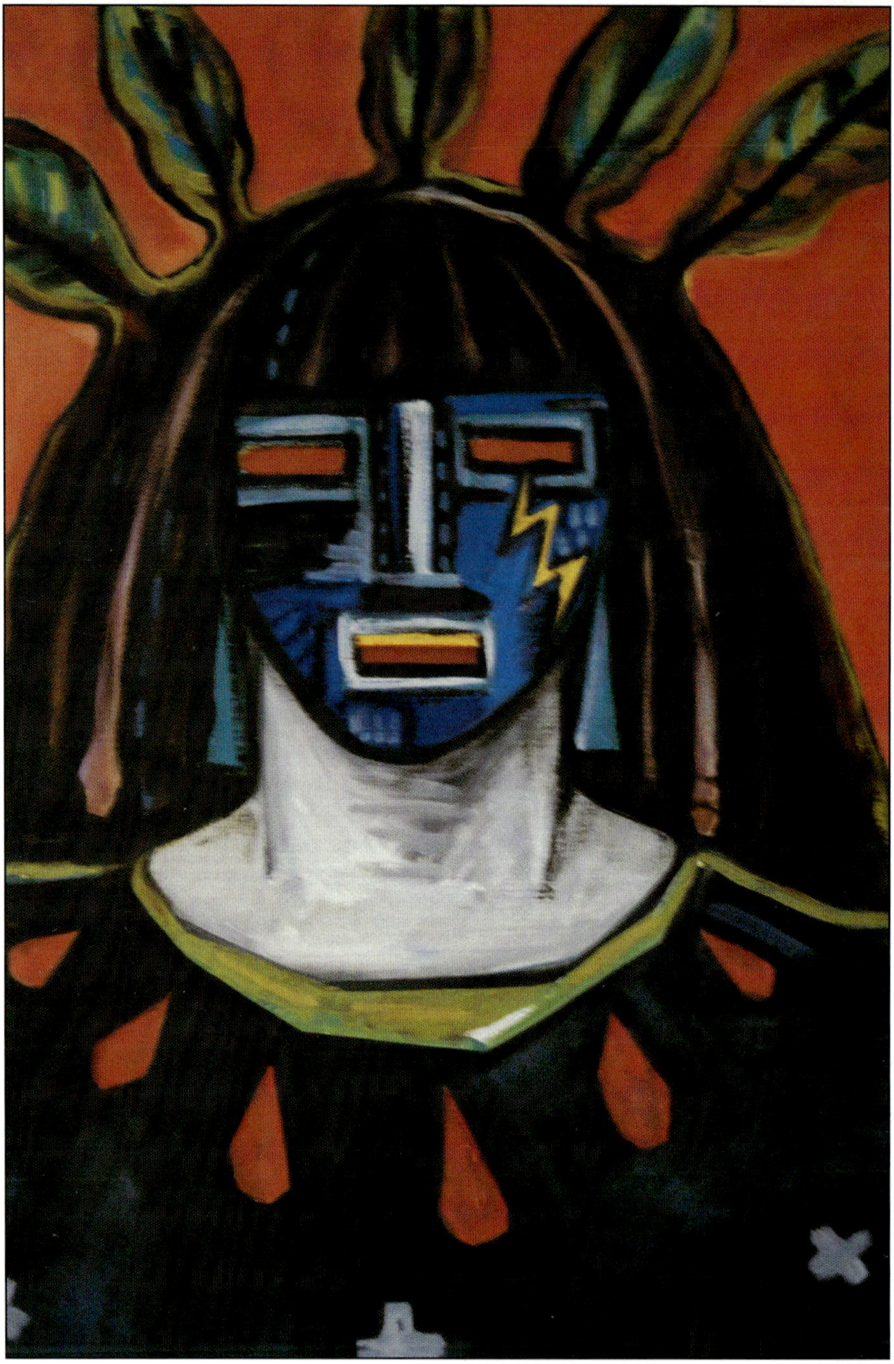

POWER MASK
1990, oil on canvas, 24" x 30"

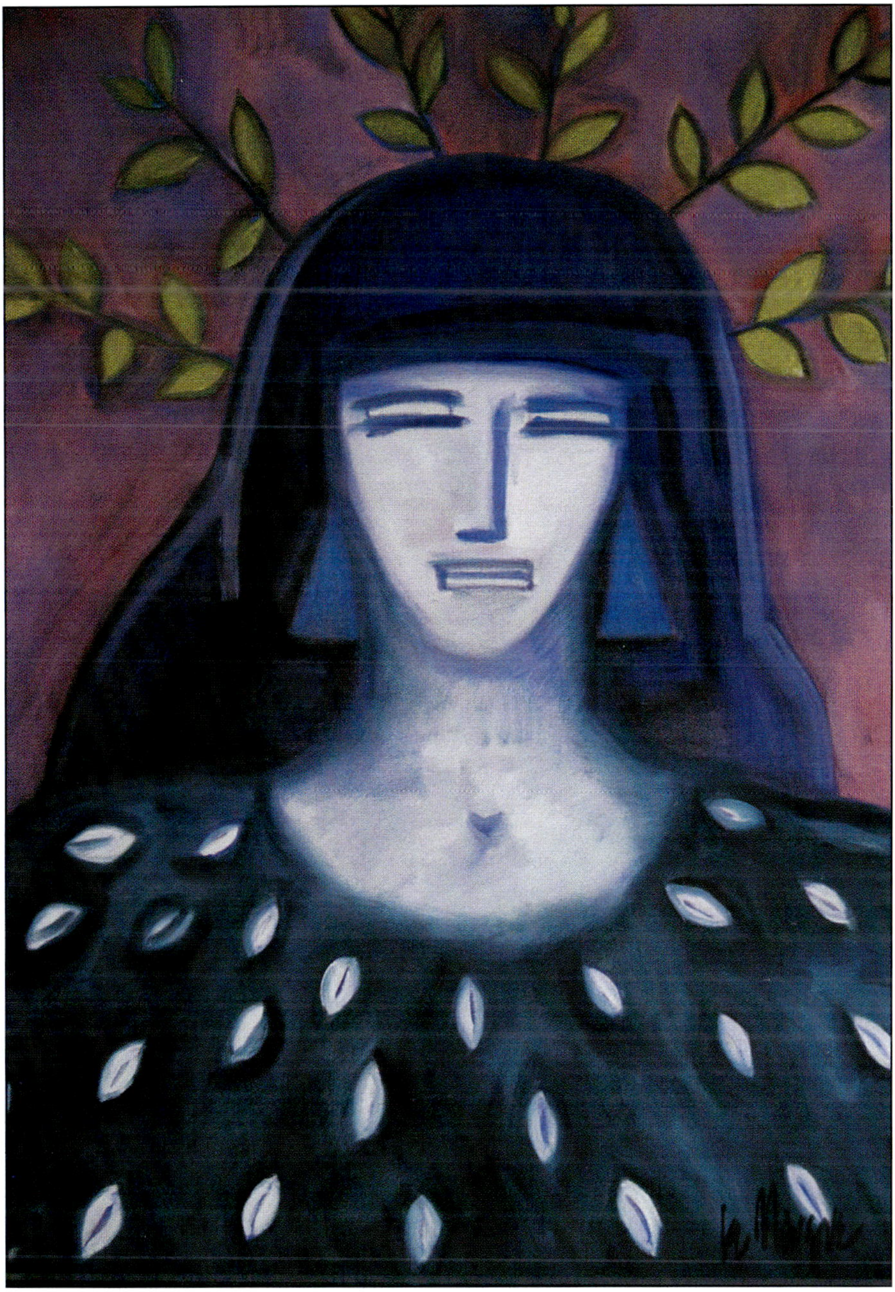

PRIMAVERA
1993, oil on canvas, 24" x 30"

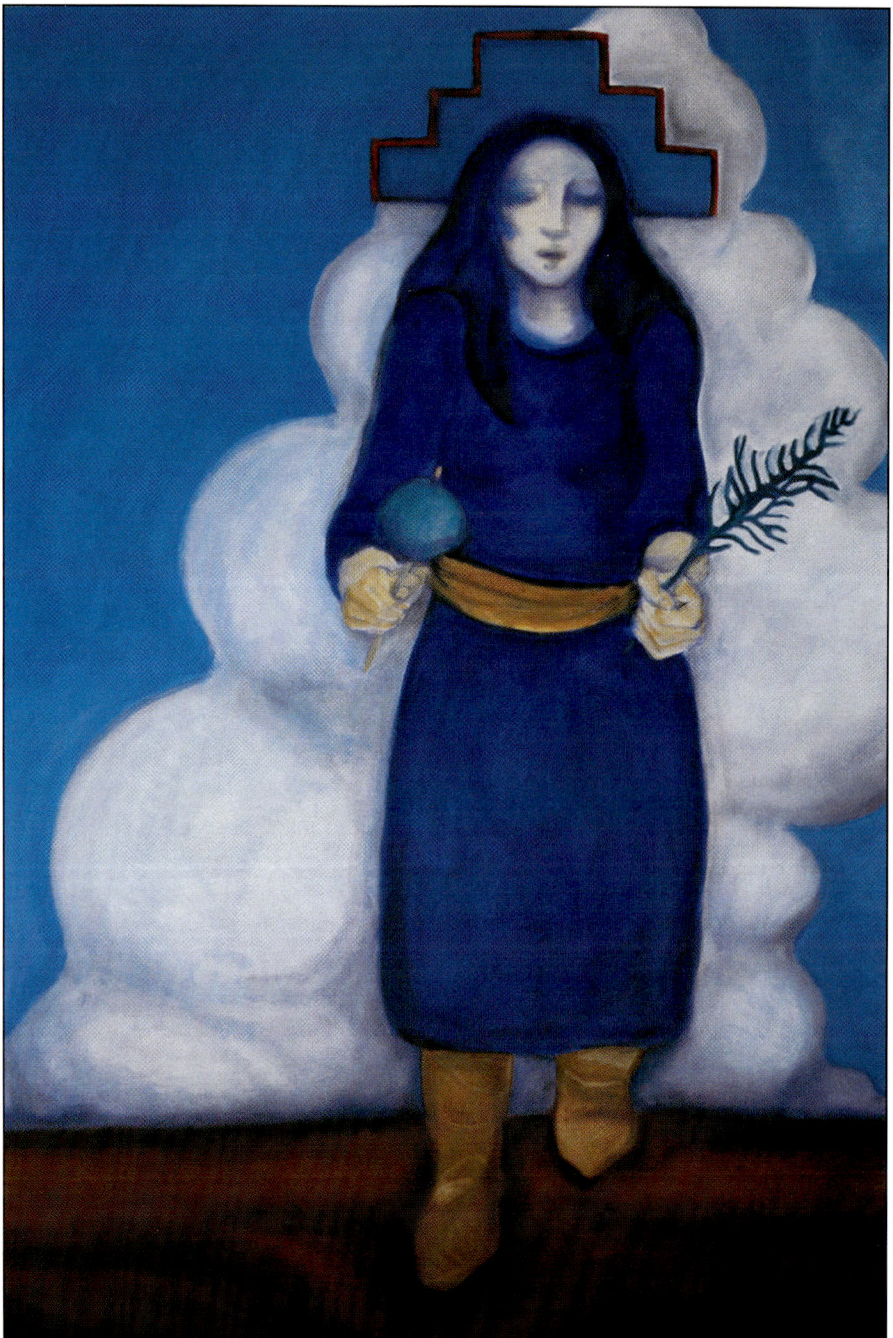

SHE BRINGS THE RAIN
1991, oil on canvas, 5' x 6'

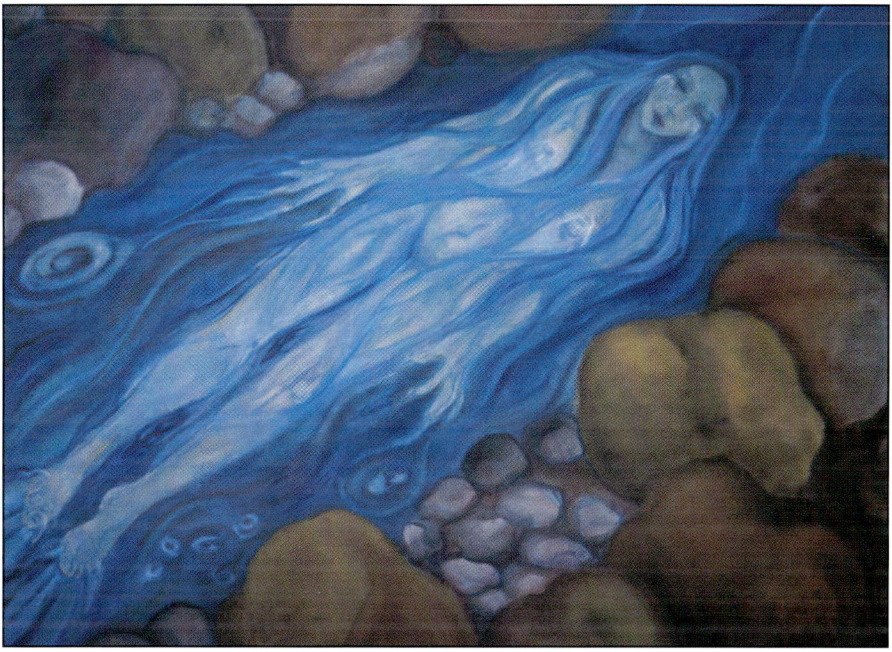

THE WOMAN WHO IS THE RIVER
1985, oil on canvas, 5' x 4'

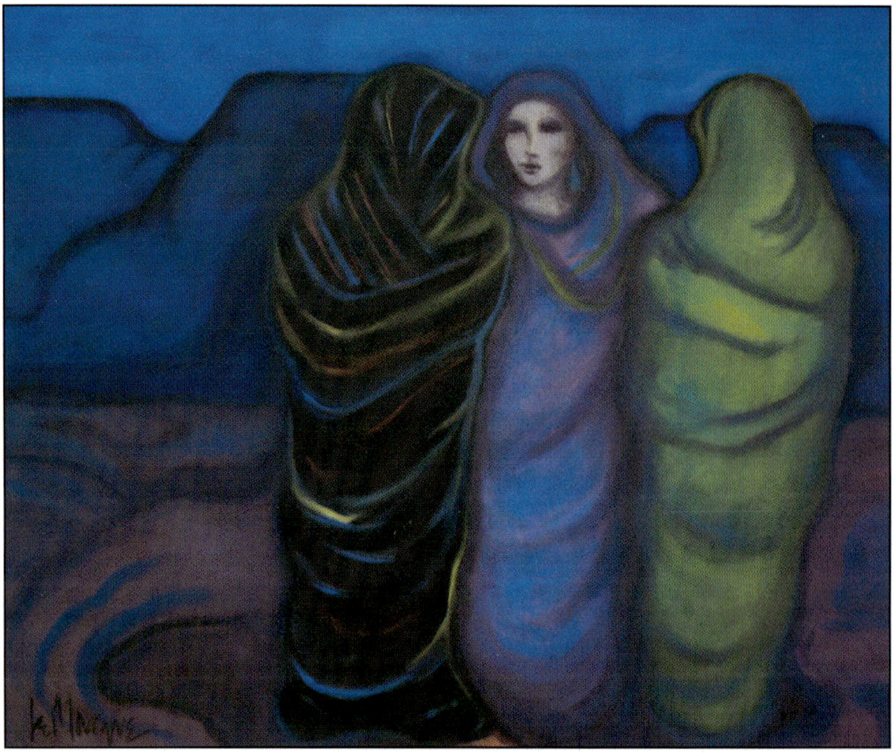

TRES MUJERES
1993, oil on canvas, 48" x 40"

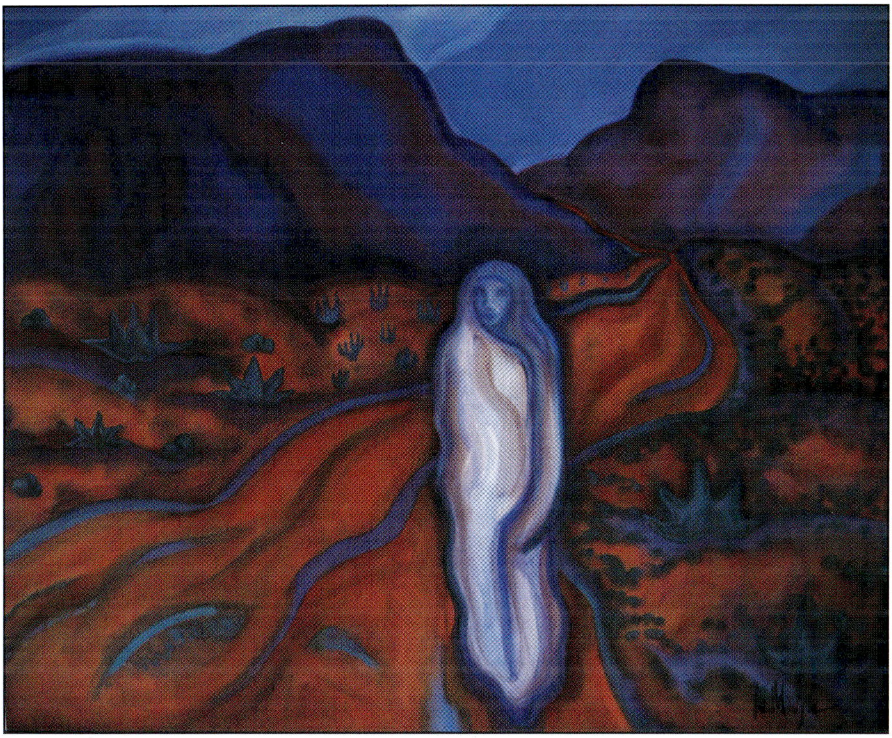

LA VIAJERA
1993, oil on canvas, 48" x 40"

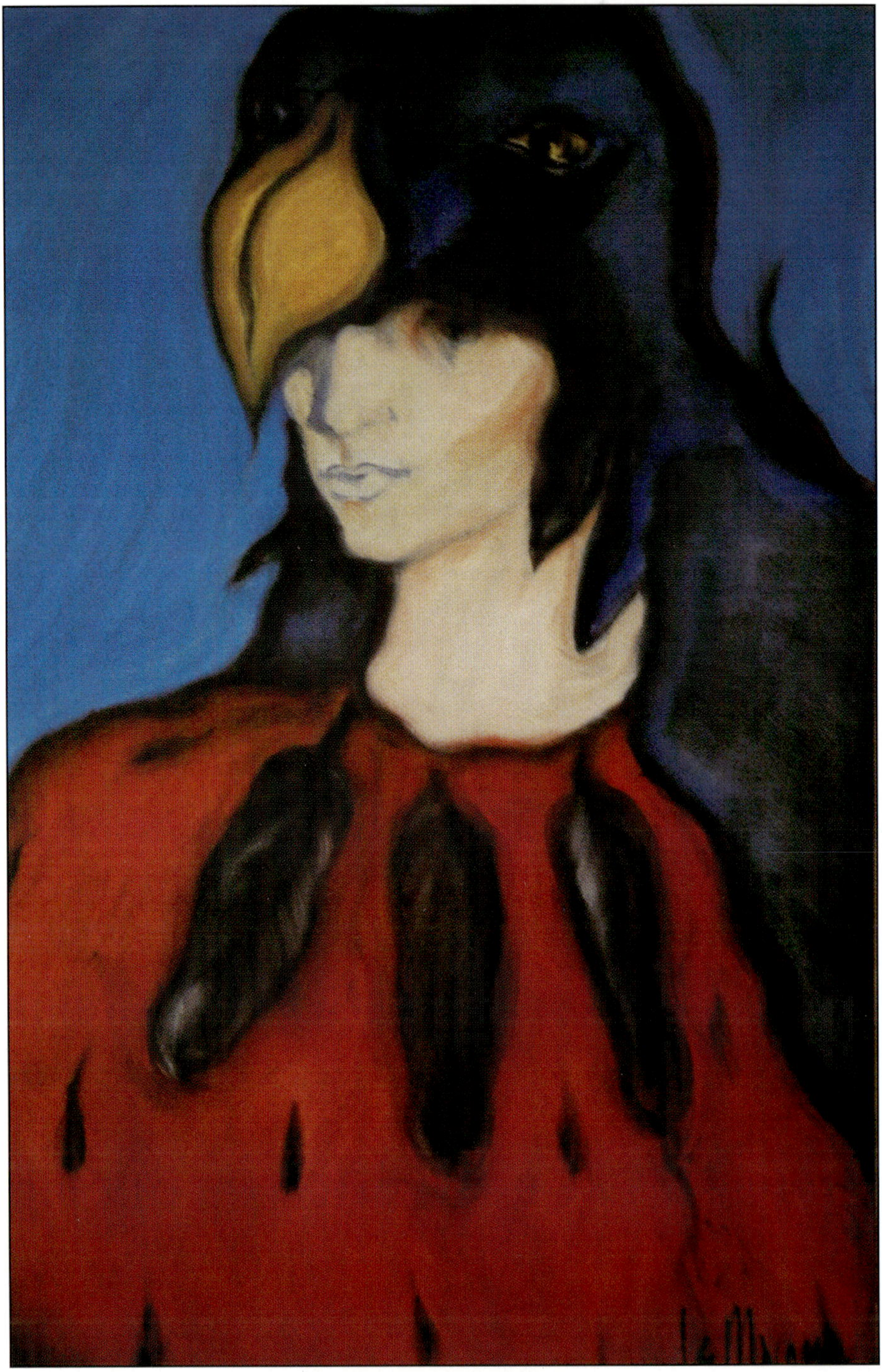

CROW WOMAN
1991, oil on canvas, 24" x 30"

Here in coyote country, residents are strongly advised to keep their cats indoors, even in broad daylight. But I cannot bright myself to do it—it would be like tethering a bird. If all cats were living in temples, as they were meant to be, perhaps things would be different. But they are not, and cats as we know them will raise the devil until he lets them out. If you have ever lived with a cat box in bloom, you might agree with them. Even if the house is surrounded by a ring of fire and a moat swarming with alligators, the cat must be let out!

A few days ago I located the International Star Registry and had a star named in honor of my mother. A dear friend of the family had a star named for my father soon after he died. Now both my parents are stars hunting in the skies eternally.

I told Sasha about the star-naming as we sat outside this evening praying to Father-Mother-God for our cat's welfare. After some contemplation, Sasha looked up at the sky and said, "God, bring our Puma home. Stars Dorothy June and Ferris, help our kitty find his way to us." What a tender, sensible request this was! Great navigators that they are in the sea of night, cats do let the stars guide their journeys.

Now, several hours after tucking a prayerful Sasha into bed, I am gazing at the last quarter of the equinox moon through the crooked *latillas* outside my window. She is there glimmering one moment, hidden by slats of wood the next. From where I sit watching her seductive appearances and disappearances as she follows her silvery path, the pads of prickly pear seem larger than the moon. Just as I feel the effects of the full moon in every part of my being, so do I sense a sweeping loneliness in her absence.

My loneliness for Puma, on the other hand, has just ended—fifteen minutes after I buttoned down the computer. I was sitting in my comfy chair reading when both dogs started acting weird, and there was our beloved black "question mark" sticking up above them. I grabbed his cool black body, slobbered him with kisses, and slicked his whiskers flat against the sides of his face. He is presently in cat Nirvana, purring loudly enough to wake everyone in the house.

A child's prayers have been answered. Good night, Ferris and Dorothy

June. Your granddaughter will be happy when she awakens to a small panther in her bed.

March 28, 1992

A pounding rainstorm is washing down the yucca that is about to bloom outside my window. As drops slap the desert sand, I feel reassured that the seeds we planted are profiting from this spring storm.

I am also feeling much better about the Coyote Woman painting. Even her shadow has taken on a life of its own. Tongue lolling to one side, this dark profile is reminiscent of a predator lurking just beneath the threshold of consciousness. I would not be surprised to come out one morning and find that the shadow had left on its own.

I'm glad to be almost done with *la Santa Coyote.* With a sweep of her arm, she has more than once torn down faulty structures in my life. Ruthless Changer of Lives, please leave me a little something—a robe, a car, some paints, a dog, the people I love—for a few more years before bringing my life down in flames. When that time comes I will, like the Queen of Swords, wield my machete as you direct, slashing.

I'm going to start a painting of a weird bird that has popped out onto the sketch pad—a peyote bird that arrived sans peyote. Already I've prepared a four-by-four-foot canvas to paint it on, even though this image has little to do with the direction of my work. Painting images that make no sense is a healthy endeavor. Artists frequently become trapped into painting only "meaningful" work, whereas very often the most fruitful elements come from simply noodling around in a sketch pad, with no thought to the end product.

Later this week I'm expecting Lori, an old friend and new student, to arrive from California for three days of painting. We'll work in the studio in three-hour blocks. Submersion is the optimal approach to art—hardly anything is more transformative.

Because Lori and I have had painful conflicts over the years, this meeting will be more than an art lesson; it will be a healing of old wounds. We were very close before our falling out, and since then, many lives have passed for us both. Fierce interpersonal conflict of this sort is common among people in recovery. A hidden storehouse of unresolved mother-goo and father-goo almost always splatters on us when we've become too close. To accelerate my growth, I usually wait for the "radiation level" to drop, then initiate contact again—sometimes to make amends, more often simply to clear my books of accounts that have gone bad. Until they are cleared, there's just so far I can travel before having to go back and unhook myself from the barbed wire.

April 4, 1992

Lori has arrived, and today we went for a hike in Sabino Canyon, where a blanket of yellow desert marigolds covered each field and mountain in our range of vision. Everywhere, little suns on earth were following the path of their father across the sky. Yellow, it seems, is yellower this year, which makes me think something inside me has changed. This phenomenon reminds me of the way the rolling green hills around San Luis Obispo looked the spring after my father died. The green of the grass was so bright that my eyes ached as I walked along the darkened edges of the underworld. But I needed that green then just like I now need the little yellow suns.

As soon as Lori and I reached the canyon, we took off our shoes and socks to ford a stream. The water was so cold that our feet throbbed, but even so, it felt good to be barefoot outdoors once again. Our eyes rejoiced, too, for the earth was bursting with blue and purple lupine, magenta penstemon, poppies hiding here and there, and the yellow flowers circling each bush and climbing up the sides of every cliff.

Lori and I talked endlessly, catching up as well as comparing notes on life and death. We also spoke of the changes we've undergone in our bodies and our beings as a result of growing older. In the end we concluded that although our bodies have not been revivified via silicone or collagen, we feel far better about ourselves than we ever did and we like who we are more than ever before. There is consolation after all for what Bob calls "the sagging and bagging, the hanging and dragging."

April 7, 1992

I woke up early today, nervous about a radio interview scheduled for late morning. While I was preparing in my usual way—painting and writing—who should come out on paper to help me but the Crow Mother kachina! At first I could not understand why I was drawn to yet another image from Native American spirituality, but then I remembered my brother telling me about a year ago that our great-grandmother was Sioux. That, I figured, was why these images were burning like signal fires in my soul, and I decided to welcome the wisdom, strength, and guidance of the entities.

Fascinated by her enigmatic mask, I made a study for Crow Mother. Then I stretched a big canvas for her and invited her to come. Now the peyote bird painting, a strong and strange piece, stands complete, and Crow Mother is coming to the fore.

In two days I'm scheduled to do a TV show for our public broadcasting station. Writing a book has made me a much more public person than I want to be. Cranked up, excited, and scared about all this publicity, I spent some time last night on the phone with Jeanne. "Tell me again it's okay that I don't do a hard sell, that I don't push myself in everyone's face," I pleaded.

"Oh," Jeanne said, "there's a book you should read by this woman who's an artist—Tina Le Marque. She says it's okay, very convincingly."

I persisted: "Tell me it's okay that I'm not in a traditional gallery."

"Yes, it's okay. Just go about your job—which is fitting yourself to be of maximum service to God—and God will in turn provide whatever you need."

"And tell me again it's okay to just paint and paint even though my house is so brimming over with canvases I can barely navigate my way through it."

"It's your job, honey. Really, you should read that book."

Whenever I suffer from doubts about my convoluted path, I call Jeanne for a double shot of love and humor. I need to know I'm on the right path, and it helps to hear it from one who bears scars from similar wars. It gets pretty spooky out here alone.

April 9, 1992

It's after 1:00 A.M. and I'm wired. The TV crew is coming at 10:00 this morning to tape the show, so there's no way I'm going to get sleep tonight. Fortunately, the no-sleep collapse usually hits in late afternoon, and by then they'll be gone.

For now, I'm content to think about the big Crow Mother painting. She's a beauty, and ever since she began to take form, the house has been pulsating. As I started to work on her, I played CDs of my favorite flute and drum music. Then when I had most of her colors blocked in, I became acutely aware of strains of music, but what I was hearing was not coming from the CD player. Boom*boom*—Crow Mother moved off the canvas!

Following a nerve-jangling prickling sensation, my hands and arms began to tremble. I felt as though I were being pressed through the wringer of an old-fashioned washing machine as I emerged into the other world. There Crow Mother stood before me, living and breathing, whereupon I fell into a reverie, flooded away in a sensory bath. Saturating myself with the colors on my palette, I swam back and forth between worlds.

Actually, she announced her arrival two weeks ago while I was hiking with Bella in the washes by the house. Scanning the ground for inspiring junk, as I often do, I came upon a shimmery black crow-wing feather. After finding a few more such feathers, I began to actively hunt for the dead crow. At first my search turned up a rusty horse shoe; the creosote bushes yielded four more horse shoes, but no crow. Feeling discouraged, I tucked my treasures under a bush, walked with Bella all the way up the wash, and played hide-and-seek with her on our return.

Only after gathering up my loot and heading back to the hacienda did I come upon the remains of the crow—several glistening black feathers, an inhabited yet intact wing, and a head complete with a beak. I brought these gifts from the desert home and tucked the black wing behind a coyote skull, tiara fashion. The loose feathers and head are waiting to be made into a ceremonial object. The worms will have to go.

Crow is the messenger this spring. In ceremony, Crow Mother comes carrying a basket of corn and bean sprouts to start the season. I'm being swept into another growing season now, and Crow Mother is here for the planting.

Chapter 9
Coyote Laughs

Tucson, Arizona
April 14, 1992

The TV shoot went well last week. It required nearly as much work as an exhibit, and I was beside myself imagining that so many people would be able to see my paintings. The crew shot footage of me working on Crow Mother and zoomed in on most of the paintings hanging in the studio. Once the terror subsides, it's exciting to do a TV show.

As for Crow Mother, she is coming steadily, in beauty. I am purposely prolonging her arrival, perhaps because she has stepped into the place my mother once occupied, but as the Great Mother—an eternal protectress who will not wear out in my lifetime. Tomorrow is my mother's birthday, which I will no longer be celebrating on this plane.

Meanwhile, a quest is on for the right container to hold my parents' ashes, which I never did scatter last autumn; no matter where I hiked in the Catalinas, I could not find a place that seemed right. I am thinking of putting their ashes together in one vessel since these two people were married to each other on a soul level. I'm drawn to the red-and-black Casas Grandes pots, because they remind me of the earth of New Mexico, but I must find just the right one. Although people are urging me to hurry and complete this laying-to-rest process, it is really about letting go, and my heart can do no more than proceed at its own pace.

My greatest concerns these last few years have been resolved: everyone whose death I was dreading has died. Yet, although I am living in a wonderful desert house in a city that has brought me back from the Land of the Dead, I am reluctant to cast these ashes over the Sonoran Desert. Why? Perhaps because I have a premonition of imminent change. Or perhaps because while Bob and I were living in Santa Fe, Dad asked me to describe the Sangre de Cristos, and when I finished, he said maybe I could scatter their ashes there when they are both dead. In any case, until I get to a place I can call home, I cannot bring myself to cast the gray powder and grit and bits of bone that sit in two small boxes on my turquoise bookshelf.

Tucson is filled with the haunting call of mourning doves, echoing the sadness that washes over me. Their song is something I will always associate with the death of my mother—a bird woman who dreamed of gigantic waves. Perhaps it is this sort of dream that has me washed away in deep longing for Santa Fe. Sometimes it is the lilacs I miss, and the sunflowers against a heartbreakingly blue sky. At other times it is the cottonwood trees with their seeds blowing everywhere, and the red-pink earth smoldering like a woman's body in heat. I cry for Santa Fe like I cry for my dead parents.

For hundreds of years people throughout the Río Grande Valley have reported the presence of a forever-wailing wandering woman they call La Llorona (She Who Weeps). I have become La Llorona—not forever, just for now.

April 18, 1992

It's Saturday and the baby-sitter has canceled at the last minute, leaving us in the lurch. I've come into my office and barricaded the door for a few moments of writing. Bob, meanwhile, has gone off to the park with Sasha before the slide gets hot enough to fry her little backside. Why don't people plant trees around the playgrounds in this land that even in spring resembles hell in summer?

I worked some more on Crow Mother yesterday. I'm still dragging out this rendering like a book I don't want to end.

April 21, 1992

Shortly after 6:00 A.M. I was awakened from a brain-dead state by the sound of Brujo throwing up. Leaping from my bed like a warrior, I somehow managed to devise strategies of sheer genius to get the dog out. Victorious, I slipped back into bed, only to realize that I could not fall asleep.

So I padded down the hall to the office, shushing the dogs as they made their morning seal-noises. Then Bella got ready to throw up. Nonetheless, I somehow slipped into a poetic mode and saw the beauty of the morning.

As the hours passed, the simplest activities brought intense pleasure and deep meaning. It seemed the height of sensuality to take a shower. I reveled in the richness of the bar of soap and the soothing pressure of the water. I took time to put on various lotions and oils, then doused myself with the scent of sandalwood, which warmed me. After leaving the bathroom, I lit a stick of piñon incense, opened the shutters, and drank in the golden light angling through the cactus.

In the garden, stems are topped by fat buds waiting for the right moment to burst open. Out in the desert wilds, thousands of cactus have begun their astonishing spring display. Rich yellow and vermilion flowers perch like exotic birds on the prickly pear. Delicate magenta cups balance on the most forbidding cactus like butterflies touching down only for a moment. I used to drive a long way to witness this scene; now I need only glance up from whatever I'm doing in the house, or walk down the driveway for the paper. The desert is in a state of riot.

It is these moments of heightened awareness that I work so hard to attain. Each time I am able to experience my life while it's happening, I feel close to God and loved.

Bob just stopped in for a visit. Since Sasha is still asleep, we took a rare opportunity to gaze out the window together. Hardly ever do we get to take in the desert without the kid coming in to tell us she's starving and wants buckwheat cakes "right now." I also attribute this peaceful interlude together to the fact that Bob has settled down considerably, perhaps because he went for a little therapeutic tune-up. Now that the rage he stored up while caring for my mother is bursting out under the holding power of a therapist, things between us are the way they should be—loving and harmonious once again.

May 7, 1992

We've just come back from a challenging, exhausting, yet gratifying week-long workshop in Mazatlán. The first movement session we did there had a decidedly Fellini-esque quality as we danced to a classical tape that David, our tour leader, had brought with him for the occasion.

A few of the participants were surprised by the art that came out of them over the course of the week, and their pleasure was beautiful to see. Pulling out images is difficult for people who have not had nurturing experiences with their creativity, and indeed many of those who attended our workshop had experienced outright pain or trauma while experimenting with art, music, poetry, dance, or song. They are among the legions of art illiterates and phobics produced by our cultural values.

Very few students in United States school systems have had a favorable introduction to art, much less to its uplifting, spiritual, and mind-expanding effects. While working with my students, I encounter numerous "land mines" left behind by their earlier experiences. Our sessions in Mazatlán were no different; Bob and I strove mightily to get past the minefields to a place where participants could allow themselves to enjoy playing with color and seeing what comes out, whether or not it is "salable" or even "hangable."

These sessions left me more depleted than others. By 9:00 P.M. each day I was destroyed—in part because of all the suppressed emotion, yet also because tension between the men and women was siphoning off everyone's energy. To sustain my energy reserves I had to continually remind myself that I was not obligated to participate in the power struggles.

My spirit was restored when, during one session, I found that I had grown coyote ears and had a long bushy tail that swung as I trotted around the circle of dancing men and women. In my mind I was circling overhead, disentangling myself from the group, when along came Sister Coyote. "Where did these ears and tail come from?" I asked her. "You like those?" she replied. "Hey, some of these people you're dancing with are terminally stuck, and there's nothing you can do for them! Concentrate on the ones who want to change. Some will get the message, and others aren't meant to."

"What about feeling so drained at night?" I asked. "Don't worry, little sister," Coyote Woman said. "People try to load you down with their leaden baggage. All you have to do is take each package for a moment, then pass it over to me. I'll take their stuff and bury it. Now, follow me. The ones who are meant to come along will find their way. As you're dancing, keep your ears erect and your nose pointed in the direction you want to go. Nice tail!" That was when the tide turned for us all.

The Thursday painting group met today—a great relief after the strains of the workshop. As the women painted, I finished Crow Mother, all the while plugging into the image and feeling strength flow into me. There is a groundedness to her, a stability. She is the great feminine mystery that stops me from missing my mother like a "lost child" or a helpless orphan.

May 8, 1992

A beautiful piece of flute music by Carlos Nakai is curling out of my stereo. The tones have an otherworldly quality, transporting me beyond my office walls. A moment ago, while listening to the music, I caught a glimpse of myself in the mirror that used to belong to my mother, and there I saw a face superimposed over mine. I see that I am shifting. What now? Who next? This ceaseless rearranging of features reflects the unsettled quality of my life.

Sunday is Mother's Day, an occasion that brings memories of my mother, who always insisted that I not buy her a gift. Each year, she would scoffingly reiterate that Mother's Day was cooked up by greeting card companies to boost their business, and doing things for her or making things for her would be more acceptable than a present. By my teenage years the enigma was solved: having become tender of the family rose bushes, I began giving my mother roses I had grown myself. Gigantic bouquets of blooms filled the house with rose perfume.

Mother's Day also brings back memories of my first celebration of the day with Sasha, when she was three months old. We visited an art museum in Santa Fe, where she was enthralled by everything she saw. While holding her face-outward, I scanned her back and forth in front of each painting while she cooed and chattered to it. Then we returned home, where Sasha and Bob cooked a special dinner—a tradition they have carried on ever since.

I want to be real around my daughter; in turn, I am creating an atmosphere in which *she* can be real. I show my feelings openly, including my anger. I make up after I've blown up. I try to model the behavior of a healthy woman who takes care of her own needs before seeing to those of others. When Sasha gets to the mom-is-such-a-jerk stage, it will be hell for me, because she's going to have a lot of real-life weapons and ammunition. But right now, while her foot still fits in the palm of my hand, we laugh and cry together. She is my true Mother's Day gift.

May 19, 1992

I am dangerously short on free time—aimless time in which to listen to the quiet of the desert, or lie still in the hammock gazing at the intense yellow of the palo verde blossoms against the blue of the Catalinas. I've got too many appointments, too many obligations. The speed of my life is pressing my nose flat against my face.

Nor are things about to improve. My schedule over the next six months includes several radio shows, articles, and public speaking engagements. My insides panic at the prospect of performing or pretending to be someone other than who I am. To prevent my life from turning into an avalanche, I've got to set boundaries, say no when I need to. Actually, I'm already moving in that direction. Since I am currently three or four weeks behind in returning phone calls and since we receive ten to twenty calls a day, every now and then I turn the answering machine to "erase."

The greatest problem is that I am participating in a conspiracy to keep myself from writing. I stop and brew tea. I get up and go to the bathroom. I wander to another bathroom looking for dental floss. On my way back to the office, I sort laundry, load the washing machine, and scrape the dryer's lint screen minutely clean. Then once the wash is going, I remind myself to clear off my desk, return whatever phone messages have slipped through, and answer at least some of the letters stacked in my cubby hole. Although convinced that I am being efficient and keeping the house clean and my life in working order, I nearly always succeed in derailing myself.

May 23, 1992

Yesterday I went out into the desert on a horse, along with a group of others. The ride was slow and plodding, but the desert was glorious, and the smell of the horses even more so. We rode for about an hour and a half, some of which I spent jotting down in a small writing pad little thoughts and phrases that came to me. I also thought about how I wanted to spend the evening, as Bob was out of town. Sasha and I would watch the stars until her bedtime, I decided, at which point I would write nonstop.

It's funny, I thought, that even as a young child I was never satisfied with activities others seemed to like. I would put on classical music and draw. I read continually. A chronic insomniac at age five, due to Tedral—the debilitating asthma drug I was on—I walked the dogs secretly at night. I danced under the moon when it was full, communed with all manner of spirits, and carried on a deep friendship with my long-dead grandmother Mimi.

Since then, I realized, my interests haven't changed much. When the house is quiet, I find it natural to turn inward. Hence, the prospect of a night at home writing filled me with excitement; there was nothing I would rather be doing.

When Sasha was tucked in for the night, I followed through with my plan. Right away I began contemplating my next painting. It may well be another self-portrait; the last one I painted appears on the cover of *Warrior Woman,* completed a year ago, and I am no longer the woman I was then.

May 27, 1992

I've given many private painting lessons this week. And although this morning's student canceled at the last minute and my easel is set up to go, I don't feel like painting. Actually, over the past few days I've been using my free time for writing. As a painter *and* writer, I always have an alternate path to follow when I lose my way in one of these worlds.

During lessons and workshops I've been halfheartedly fiddling with a smaller version of Coyote Woman that's been languishing on my easel for quite some time. She became too pretty, a little boring—though she's got the face she said was hers this time. Yesterday I smudged the features just enough to give her a certain ambiguity; the eyes are now shadowy, a little out of focus. It's a simple painting with limited colors, and I like it better than when it was too perfect, but I'm still not sure it's the real thing.

June 1, 1992

I have started work on a self-portrait. When I stand back to survey it from across the room, I see silver hairs sticking up from the bangs. While painting them, I was catapulted back to the time I first cut bangs. I was living with my husband Philippe when one afternoon while he was out, I stepped up to the mirror and snipped a little fringe of hair across my forehead. When he came home, we sat down for a conversation, and partway into it, he abruptly reached over and flicked my wispy bangs with a pencil. "What is this?" he asked, his voice dripping with ridicule. "Bangs. I cut some bangs," I told him. "They look really dumb and stupid," he said. Over the next fifteen minutes he periodically reached over with the pencil and knocked my new bangs around—in a rare display of nastiness. A burst of clarity revealed that I was not about to play doormat to him.

Now, fifteen years later, I still have bangs. There are more of them; untouched-up silver hairs are threaded among them; I am in a second marriage; and I don't tolerate people trying to control my actions or my appearance. I am, as Bob says, "a spectacle in my own right."

The silver hairs I see in the painting, as in the mirror, tell me two things. First, that lifetimes have gone by since I was a defiant fifteen year old stepping off a jet from Paris smoking a small cigar and wearing no bra, much to the horror of my perplexed hometown boyfriend. And second, that my rebellious nature remains unmitigated.

June 10, 1992

The moon is getting fuller, as am I—uncomfortably so. It's 3:00 A.M. and something is sorely troubling me. I feel like I have horrible PMS, but I do not; rather, I am stretched out and stressed out. Perhaps writing will reveal the source of the problem.

One difficulty is my increasingly public life. Public living is draining and exhausting. All the TV shows, book signings, presentations, and large workshops I've completed suggest that I can be extroverted at times, yet I am alternately and equally introverted. For my most recent public appearance I showed up, but I was writhing; I would much rather have been working at my desk or painting in my studio. It appears that I am spending so much time around humans that I've been distracted from my quiet spiritual center. Life these days is way too busy for me to hear the inner voices.

Contributing to my discomfort is the presence of yet another houseguest. Ever since my mother died, I have been like a cat on a hot tin roof about extraneous people sharing my living space, and there have been swarms of them. I feel guilty about wanting to strangle people I care about, and I'm angry that Bob doesn't listen when I say, "I need to be alone. Shut the door—quit inviting the world to our house." He nods and proceeds to extend an invitation to "just one more person." I consent, saying, "Sure, he needs a place to stay. Let him come." But if I don't start saying no, there's going to be nothing left of Tina.

What ails me is that I am lonely for myself, my solitude, the simple life I knew in Santa Fe. The remedy is spiritual: I must clean my emotional house by going out into the desert and sitting on the bare earth, sweeping the floor, and praying. God, just put me where you want me to be. Help me say no, de-clutter, and refuse the call to frenzied problem solving. Show me what you want me to do. Fill up my life with more of you—just you and your simple ways. Help me know that I don't have to be Mother Teresa to win your love.

God has guided me before. When I was twenty-eight years old, my sister Sharon told me she had cancer and, short of a miracle, was going to die. I wondered if I could live through her dying, if our family would recover from the blow, if we could ever be happy again. The months that followed taught me that in the midst of the most awful crisis I could feel good and have fun; I could feel good while others did not; and feeling good was a matter of survival. Realizing how important it was to live when people I cared about were dying, I learned to shift into living in the moment—initially to make it through Sharon's death, and eventually for the sheer joy of it.

Somewhere along the way I figured out that "God's will" for me was to be happy. Imagine that—a mandate for joy from the highest office in the land! And so I learned to enjoy life; even tears had their sweetness. Better yet, I found that I don't need to obliterate myself in order to love another person. In short, the most important lesson I gleaned while coming out the other side of Sharon's death was to choose to be happy whenever I can, and that is the capacity I must now reinvigorate.

June 11, 1992

What is making me so damn uncomfortable? I have not been this wormy for a long time. Something feels drastically wrong, and I don't yet know what it is. What I do know is that I am angry; I want to be left alone; I am easily jangled; the house is too busy and noisy; and I want to retreat deep inside myself. I suppose I am still allowing myself to become overextended and overly tired.

Because I feel about as bad as I did right after my mother died, I'm guessing that some of this discomfort is another layer of grieving. The sadness comes up like that—a shadowy form swimming slowly to the surface. Every few months since she's died, I've hit a new layer of grief.

June 14, 1992

Something odd happened the other day. I asked Sasha to come in and watch TV on my bed. While flicking through the channels for a kid show, I quickly passed by the Clint Eastwood movie *Bronco Billy,* which unbeknownst to her, my dad edited. "I want to watch that one!" she squealed gleefully. Transfixed, she watched it through to the end.

As soon as *Bronco Billy* was over, I ran through the other channels until a darkly lit western came on. "I want to watch that one!" Sasha exclaimed once again. It was *Joe Kidd,* another film my dad cut, and not one that would attract the attention of a four year old. But something pulled her right in—tribal memories, no doubt.

June 17, 1992

The voltage that runs through me when I begin to write is frightening. It is as though a gate opens and a herd of horses rip and snort their way out.

Yesterday I had one of those deflating experiences that artists know so well. In the morning a friend called to inform me that the salespeople at a local store specializing in beautiful Southwestern items had just sold a large painting from its window and that the buyer was looking for a special piece to replace it. My friend described my work to her and she was very interested in seeing it.

After picking Sasha up from school, I drove to the store, hoping to see the space so I would know what kind of art to present. While Sasha played quietly under a table, I asked to see the buyer. "Hi, I'm Tina Le Marque," I said to the buyer. "I'm a local artist. My friend told me you were interested in finding a large painting to display in your window." "No," the woman replied, "I'm not looking for anything." She clearly had nothing more to say.

I couldn't get out of there fast enough. After finding a nearby pay phone, I called Bob. "I'd rather burn my paintings than go into one more store or gallery to see about showing my work. They act as if I'm an intruder asking to borrow money from them. I'll be damned if I ever subject myself to that again," I told him, sobbing.

After hanging up, I looked at my daughter's tousled blonde hair and remembered what was truly important: my family, my individuality, and the creativity I have been given. My life is full of love, I reminded myself, and although I am deadly embarrassed to have been given the boot, in the grand scheme of the universe that store doesn't have much meaning.

Turning a corner, Sasha and I stopped to toss shiny pennies into a fountain and listen as they plunked into the water, glimmering coppery against the bright cobalt-blue tile. I examined the odd shapes the water made as it shot upward and stood for a split second against the sky. "No matter who says I can or can't show my work on their walls, I'm still an artist," I told myself. "It's a cellular-soul matter, not a gallery one. The simple fact is that galleries don't create artists; what makes an artist is a vision and an action taken to materialize that vision, or an ability to feel and an intense need to express those feelings." Throwing coins in the fountain didn't take away the pain, though it did realign my perspective.

June 25, 1992

We have returned from a great adventure. Following our friends Linda and Martin to their favorite camping place, Bob, Sasha, and I spent three blissful days on the banks of the Black River.

Linda and Martin have two children: Elaina, who is Sasha's best friend, and her brother Nicky. Within five minutes of arriving at the campsite, the three kids threw their clothes into the bushes and began digging in the black earth. At one point, Sasha and Elaina perched atop a fallen tree that lay about six and a half feet off the ground, delirious with their heightened perspective. All three kids then proceeded to collect pinecones, mash flowers, study worms, and slather themselves with mud from head to toe—an adornment that lasted for the remainder of our trip.

Linda and I cooked for hours each day. The rest of the time we spent eating and lying in hammocks. The absence of phones, answering machines, mail deliveries, and other screaming, buzzing, and ringing intrusions provided the simplicity I so badly needed. Amid this glorious interlude of unplanned time and drifting space, stirring the beans became a meaningful experience.

In the mornings and after lunch we all walked in the river. From time to time we would lie down and let the current carry us along, or throw rocks, or gaze upriver at the unspoiled beauty of the rippling stream. We laughed each time a crawfish shot backward through the water.

Come afternoon, the sky would suddenly turn black and drop buckets of rain. On the second afternoon of menacing blackness, Sasha and I retreated to our tent, where the *tappity-tap* of drops on the canvas hypnotized us into a deep sleep.

At night I dreamed. The first night I dreamed that the clearing where we had pitched our tents was teeming with people, whose presence I could still feel upon awakening. The second night I dreamed that I was gazing into the Black River, where I saw a motionless ornamental fish illuminated by a shaft of late afternoon sunlight. The fish—the emperor's koi—was breathtakingly beautiful; it was white and rich red speckled with flecks of real gold. I knew immediately that I had been shown a wise ancient being of immense value, a treasure of the deepest waters.

I am grateful that my dreams are once again vivid and meaningful, and that they are now leading me to the deep waters of my spirit. Although for many months I was disappointed and lonely upon awakening from seemingly dreamless sleeps, I am now convinced that they were *not* dreamless, that the repairs my psyche needed were taking place beneath the threshold of consciousness. Certainly, I missed the cryptic "letters" from the dark continent, yet I trust my inner process.

Not only did my dream life flourish during this three-day respite, but my marriage did as well. Rarely do Bob and I get to travel to places where no one is waiting for us to perform or say something profound. Relieved to have nothing expected of us, we wallowed in aimlessness, walked shoeless in the mud, drooped into our hammocks, and collapsed at nightfall beside a huge bonfire blazing beneath a star-filled sky.

Chapter 10

Visiting the Black Madonna

Tucson, Arizona
June 28, 1992

Yesterday was especially rich. First thing in the morning I gave a painting lesson to a young girl of seven who likes to come and make pictures. When she gets hungry, we nibble on cheese and apples. She talks about her garden and her dogs, plays her grandmother has taken her to, and paintings in her grandma's house. She talks a lot, yet she is a lovely little spirit.

After she left, two women arrived from the "clan of Nan," a dear friend in recovery who lives in Los Angeles. When I was running Felicity House, a recovery home for women in Los Angeles, Nan was the first person I interviewed to come into the house. Sullen and reluctant to step inside, she was dragged in by a sister-in-law who seemed eager to be rid of her.

At the time of her arrival, Nan was devastated by a sad divorce, a recently severed relationship with a lover, and the death of her best friend. Moreover, her mother had just survived a bout with breast cancer, which we both intuitively knew would some day come back to take her. As for me, it was my first day on the job. I was still absorbing the shock of my sister's death and walking in the shadow of my own death and dismemberment. Not surprisingly, Nan and I spent many afternoons wrapped around each other crying in her attic room. The tears that flowed so freely healed us both, and the immediate sense of sisterhood we felt grew into many years of closeness and mutual support.

Even though Nan is now ten years sober and I am living 500 miles away from her, we are still in regular contact by phone. So when the two women appeared at my door explaining that Nan sponsors them in a 12-step program in Los Angeles, I greeted them as grandchildren. We drank iced tea and jumped into the pool, after which they regaled me with stories they had heard about my work with Nan and words I had uttered to her many years ago.

I was moved by their visit. It seems there's a forest of women growing in Los Angeles from selfish work I undertook to keep myself sober—from seeds I planted to save my own life and earth I turned to claw my way into the human race.

At noon I raced to a workshop on the Black Madonna given by Tucson-based teacher and poet Joy Oshun. After careful preparation, twenty-five of us danced in the dark for two and a half hours. Writhing down through the earth, I danced toward the Black Madonna, she who gives birth to the divine within the human. Soon I arrived at a clearing where I saw my mother lying dead, and racked with grief I danced on. A snake, coyote, tree, bird, and the Black Goddess—I danced them all. Still reeling when I returned home, I flung myself into the pool again. The chill slap of the water on my skin, the clouds sailing overhead, the vultures wheeling, the blueness of the water, and the movement of light beneath its surface all added to the kaleidoscopic effects of the workshop. For hours images, tears, and laughter bubbled up from the deepest caverns in me.

Bob and Sasha were waiting inside for me. Once again, as so often before, we took up a conversation that has no tangible beginning or end: we shared our feelings about staying in Tucson as opposed to putting down roots somewhere else, about the calling of our hearts. This conversation usually starts off with the words "I need to talk about something," "This doesn't feel right," "I wonder if we . . . ," "I feel a change coming," or "I'm having dreams about big waves." More often than not, it ends with visions of a moving van roaring up the driveway.

This time, fresh from the Black Madonna workshop and my dip in the pool, I spoke of being "reassigned"—a familiar prompting that tells me something is not working, or does not feel right. Surrendering to a power greater than myself, I usually step to the Jumping Cliff and ask aloud, "Where do you want me? What do you want me to do when I get there?" I used to stand at the cliff's edge alone, but now I have Bob and Sasha as companions.

During our talk, my friend Beth called from Idyllwild, California, to report that a meeting participant had just used the term "divine discontent," and she thought I'd appreciate the expression. Upon hanging up, I announced to Bob, "I used to think of being reassigned, but now I believe it's *divine discontent* that moves me from one life to the next." I was glad to have a better name for it.

July 1, 1992

I am in a state of profound turmoil, and so is Bob. This morning I woke him up, asking, "It isn't me, is it? You love me, right? You don't want to get away from me, do you?" Although I hate to expose my insecurities, I needed reassurance—I needed to know things were okay between us. The cause of his agitation, he said, was not me.

A giant change seems to be coming. I prattle on internally, wanting to know what it will bring and how things will turn out in six months, one year, two years. I want to know that Sasha is going to be all right and that we'll make wise choices for her. Each time I complete another cycle of this depleting inner chatter, I come back to the bottom line: "God, where do you want me?"

When I am talking to God, I am not speaking to God the Father or God the Mother, or a man with a beard, or even Michelangelo's dynamic intercessor. I am instead conversing with the force in nature that knows how many petals belong on a sunflower and when the tides will roll in and slide out; I am talking to the source of all art, healing, and growth. In choosing to serve this power, I know in my gut that no matter what happens I will end up on the right path, and that whatever is taken from me will be replaced with something better.

So here I am waiting for a postcard from God, telling me, "Go there. Do this." I'm listening hard and making a superhuman effort to stay in the moment, to live as if no avalanche was about to alter the course of my life one more time.

In a few minutes one of my favorite art students, Shelby, will be here. We painted together in Kingman when she was a little kid and already showing signs of being a "born artist," but I haven't seen her in over a year. To continue our artistic camaraderie, her parents are bringing her here for a few days of painting. I wonder how much she has changed now that she's on the cusp of adolescence.

July 2, 1992

Shelby the Tall has been here and painted. I could hardly believe the transformation she has undergone; she towers over me and spews forth poignant observations about people. It is a gift to witness a wise little girl growing into a smart and savvy young woman—a creature of beauty both inside and out.

My turmoil has announced its origins. Just before Shelby arrived, I heard myself saying on the phone, for the umpteenth time, "Something's going on. I'm crazy as a loon. I don't know what it is." As the words were leaving my mouth Bob, from across the kitchen, remarked, "Yes, you do. You know exactly what's going on."

His simple statement hit me like a slap across the face. Yes, I realized, I do know what's going on: I have been shadow dancing with myself, for I am coming unstuck from Tucson. As my emotional and psychic anchors lift from the Sonoran desert, I know in my heart that New Mexico is what I'm longing for.

In fact, we will soon be leaving for a six-day visit to Santa Fe. Friends have invited us to stay at their house, but I wonder if they really have room for us. I'm planning to take a sleeping bag and curl up on their couch—or in the doghouse if need be. I'll do whatever is required to follow this "tidal pull" to visit my home.

I suspect that my husband, too, needs to go back to New Mexico—to find his writer-self. Over the past few years his connection with his creative self has diminished. Although he has completed a second book as well as several movie scripts, and is in constant demand for speaking engagements, something in his soul does not seem to be working for him here. This place sustains him between trips, but does not nurture his spirit. I know in my gut that he needs to go back to the mountains to regenerate, back to a simpler, deeper lifestyle. His pulse is a little faint here.

With Santa Fe on the horizon, this Independence Day will have new meaning now that Bob and I have said farewell to all our living parents. My earthly completion with my much loved mother and father was especially difficult since we were closer than parents and children usually are; our connection seemed to be from other lifetimes. Hence the send-off had to be done right, leaving no thoughts unspoken, no arguments unwrangled, no kisses unkissed.

Bob and I are now finished with the part of our lives most people dread: when parents become children who turn to their offspring for decision making, help, and support. Dying is not the worst of it; the biggest shock comes when these pillars of your existence are reduced to a state of helplessness, fear, and vulnerability. When people ask me what to do if their parents start to fall apart, I propose: "Be merciful and compassionate. Tell them they were good parents, even if there is only a shred of truth to it. Thank them. Tell them you love them. Not terribly far down the line, you will find yourself in their moccasins."

Santa Fe, New Mexico
July 6, 1992

Surely I have died and gone to heaven! I awoke in Santa Fe and am tentatively feeling my way along hallways of change.

Last night I had two dreams. In one, Bob and I were standing on opposite sides of a riverbank. I had been meandering beside the river for some time and knew intuitively that the whole mass of earth on the other side was about to rip loose. Suddenly seeing cracks on the ground, I yelled, "Jump!" Bob hesitated, looked at me, saw I meant it, and leaped. At that very moment the bank tore away from the land and became engulfed by the river.

In the second dream, Sasha and I were wending our way along a treacherous catwalk across an abyss. I kept telling her, "Put one foot here, the other there. Hold on to the wooden railing. Now move your foot to this spot over here." Each time she failed to follow my detailed directions for even a moment, greenish quicksand that was otherwise invisible rose up to cover her. I would turn and, using all my strength, pull her out of the greedy goo, horrified at how quickly the gaping pockets tried to swallow her.

Both dreams mirror what is happening in our lives. To make the massive transitions that have become customary in our relationship, either Bob or I have to take a blind leap of faith to the bank on which the other one is standing. Repeatedly, it seems, what appears as solid ground one moment becomes a gorge the next, as if the earth's plates themselves were moving. Sasha, for her part, has been sobbing inconsolably for an hour or two every night, equally aware that the ground is shifting and that something big is happening to Bob and me. To keep her from being sucked into quicksand as we traverse yet another passage, I must inch by inch tell her where to step. We're all hanging on to one another for dear life.

While driving through Santa Fe, I am reminded of events that previously took place at nearly every corner. To the right is the registry office where we picked up our marriage license; there on the left is the store where I received a message to go home and make love, knowing that our beloved Sasha was about to be conceived. Around that bend is the church where we were married. The best parts of my life transpired in these adobe buildings.

Wherever I turn I am embraced by someone who knows me and is delighted to hear we are coming back. But no one is as delighted as I, for this is where I lived apart from the family I was born into and where my sense of self is strongest. New Mexico is the loom for the weaving of my being.

Yes, we as a family are about to step back onto our path. Our lives have been held in trust for us here, earning emotional interest while waiting for us to find our way back, while waiting for our bodies to return to our souls. The signs are everywhere: Don't get mixed up, Hold my hand, Come back—this is where you belong.

July 7, 1992

Last night I had another vivid dream. I was walking up a long incline surrounded by woods when to my right I saw an owl. It was over three feet tall and was wearing a half-circle crown of turquoise feathers. What a weird creature this is, I thought, wondering if it was a promising sign or an omen of death. Then to my left I saw an owl that was also very tall but had salt-and-pepper coloring and large tufts of black and white feathers on its head. Walking farther up the hill I saw, amid the trees to my right, two small wolves coupling. Continuing on, I spotted to my left a full-grown buffalo that was only two feet tall. The appearance of all these creatures astounded me.

At the top of the hill I came to a room and knocked. A man I trusted was inside and, embarrassed to see me, refused to let me in. I knew he had a woman with him who was not his wife. Angry about not being let in, I walked down the hill to a cafe, stepped inside, and sat down. Soon the man came in and began telling me how happy he was that I could accept what was going on. I was so angry that I didn't tell him his behavior was insidious. As he babbled on, I got up and left.

Soon after I stepped outside, a retriever came toward me barking and snapping, which surprised me, since dogs usually love me. But this one decidedly did not, and I had to grab his lower jaw to keep him from biting me. Suddenly there appeared another snapping retriever, whose jaw I grabbed with my other hand. When a third dog came at me ready to bite, I began kicking the cafe window to let the customers know I was in trouble. But every time I started to bang on the window with my foot, the dogs tried to bite my other leg. I was terrified, and angry that the people in the cafe didn't notice the desperate straits I was in.

Then the door opened and people came pouring out. Among them was Bob, as well as a woman in high heels and a cocktail dress waiting to talk to him. He spotted her, rather than noticing my dilemma, whereupon she wrapped herself around him. At that point the dogs disappeared, and a man came over to tell me how beautiful I was. "What you see is not beauty, but rage," I bellowed.

This dream speaks to me of hostile forces in my world. I am unnerved by it.

Tucson, Arizona
July 10, 1992

Yesterday, after dropping Bob off at the Albuquerque airport for a business trip, Sasha and I continued on across the desert together. Looking up, I could see spirals of vultures coiling loosely in the crystalline sky, giving new meaning to the Patrolled by Aircraft signs.

Although long stretches of desert driving can be grueling, I love them. I turn on some music, let my mind off its leash, and "fly." I highly recommend a long car trip through great empty spaces for anyone entering a time of transition. It helps cut the mooring lines.

July 11, 1992

Last night monsoons deluged the desert, filling the air with the intoxicating smell of sky and earth undiluted by smog or gasoline fumes or expensive perfumes. It is the real smell of life, with wafts of death curling around its periphery. This death scent is part of the medley, the way the atmosphere was meant to be before people forgot and tried to run away from it.

Out my office window I see quail couples dashing about helter-skelter with babies the size of Ping-Pong balls bobbing after them like a perfectly choreographed drill team. How do they survive with us stomping about and careening around corners with no concern for the small and uninfluential? Perhaps by being endowed, in a way humans are not, with enough intelligence to stick together. Mom and dad can be trusted to do what nature intended them to do. Maybe they even have radar in their little "hats."

Off in the distance I see a solitary rabbit nibbling at a viciously spiked cactus. Now *there's* a life more parallel to ours! Eat and screw; screw and eat. All that's missing is the TV.

At the moment I am working against time, for soon Sasha will be waking up and ordering food from The Waitress. It must be the quail in me that I hear saying, "Face it, Tina. Four years old is too young to be working a gas stove and cooking scrambled eggs for the family."

Even so, quail thinking dictates that artists' and writers' kids must be trained early on in the running of the homestead. Rip those tiaras off their heads unless you want to set up shop beside the washing machine. Buy the best appliances you can, and give instructions in how to push the buttons. Already I've decorated the VCR with a round red sticker for "stop" and a square green one for "go," and Sasha knows how to operate it. She also knows how to work the microwave oven, although parental supervision is still required to make sure she does not warm up Puma.

Earlier this morning, long before thoughts of waitressing crossed my mind, I walked through the house looking at my paintings. The new version of Coyote Woman took me by surprise, for after months of struggle she has evolved into a magnificent creature. What she was wanting was a shadow, a little darkness—like the rest of us.

I'm also pleased with the most recent self-portrait. When it's in a room with company, they gaze at it and talk, conversing with the image instead of me. It's difficult to make a portrait interesting, since basically it's a severed head. A *talking* portrait, on the other hand, might be fascinating, provided that it does not have holes shot in it—an unlikely outcome for articulate self-portraits.

With thunder rolling in the distance, I've begun tying up the strands of my life in Tucson. I'm going through closets pulling out armloads of clothes that don't feel like me anymore. Boxes of books are stacking up for the used-book store. Piles of food and cookware other people can use are growing in the pantry. The furniture consignment lady is coming next week to start taking away items that don't belong to the woman I am becoming.

July 15, 1992

A few days ago I was having misgivings about moving so far from Jeanne, then yesterday I called her house to break the news to her, only to find that she was in the hospital recovering from surgery on a blocked carotid artery. Had she not caught it in time, the results would have been disastrous.

I was shaken by the thought of losing Jeanne, the person who saved my life. She was the first—and for years the *only*—person I trusted. What's more, I knew she loved me. "Honey," she said when we first met, "I don't love you because you're so cute and nice. I love you because you're rotten." Actually, I was neither cute nor nice; I was one of the walking dead. But Jeanne was not afraid of the darkness in me. When she looked into my eyes, I knew she saw the wild animal there . . . and still she loved me.

Although I am turning the wheels and gears that will move me from one life to another, I am not controlling this operation; I am merely acquiescing. It feels like Bob, Sasha, and I are on a greased cosmic slide, and the message I hear loud and clear is: "Let go of all forms of thinking and problem solving, including figuring out what to let go of. Slip into a state of powerlessness and weightlessness. Prepare for a free fall."

It's a magnetic phenomenon, this inner calling. The receiver, hard-wired into the animal part of our brains, picks up the cues: "Go here. Follow this trail. Drink from this watering hole, not the one with the bones around its banks." Now the sensors are up and running, pushing at me to break loose and go. Well-heeled and highly polished vampires are walking away with pieces of my husband, so I'm going to pack him up and take him home, where he can remember who he is. We all need to be where we can remember who we are.

I suspect that another reason we are moving is to get away from the woodpeckers. Every morning they wage psychological warfare by pecking on the metal strip along the swamp coolers and the side of the house while we are peacefully asleep. Bob has done everything in his power to refrain from bombing them with full artillery, and I have done everything in mine to protect them from his wrath.

Now, however, my job is to lighten my load. Fortunately, I know how to throw everything I neither need nor want out of my abode. And I am happy to say that Bob and I are getting along—which is equally fortunate, because over the years there's been more than one dead soldier in the sand outside my tipi.

July 17, 1992

A new student named Jeff came yesterday. Seeing immediately what a complicated knot of thought he is, I got out my watercolors, Sumi-e ink, and bamboo brushes; then I spread newspaper across the worktables and painted on big black lines. I dibbled and dabbled watercolors all around this man, making small open compartments and mazes with thick brush strokes and undiluted ink. By the end of the lesson, he was in the center of my "sand painting," which formed a giant healing circle around him.

At this point Jeff needed to talk for quite some time. Then after discharging his thoughts, he exploded into images, painting frenetically. But his head hardly gave him a moment of peace.

At last I laid down the guidelines: "I'm not going to tamper with your creative process; I'm going to assist it. I do not criticize students' work or use prearranged lesson plans. I am not going to give you photographs or assignments to work from. You'll learn to draw by opening your personal imagery closet and coming upon symbols, objects, people, and situations that are meaningful to you. Don't think—simply listen to the music. I do not want you to paint like *I* do; I want you to paint like *you* do."

Jeff had come to the studio via a new route: his lessons were a gift from his wife Karen, a local artist. Over twenty years ago he painted in college, but since then his only interaction with art has been to think about it, an act that reliably kills creative impulses. When during his lesson he let fly with perhaps fifteen variations of an extremely agitated face, his own stormy face raged under a mask of composure. "Date these pieces," he stated. "Do not throw them away." He reads biographies of the saints, he explained, whereupon I suggested that such material could make him mentally ill and sent him off to read "saint" Henry Miller.

I woke up this morning craving a cup of Chinese keemun tea. For years I have been a tea addict, ordering blends by the case from California or Louisiana since my taste in tea, as in all things, runs toward the exotic. It annoyed me to wake up wanting something I didn't have. "It's on its way," I told my inner spoiled brat. "Now, drink this English breakfast variety and go sit at the computer." Which is exactly what I did.

I then called Jeanne's house and was delighted to hear her answer the phone sounding strong and feisty. The doctors will operate on her other carotid artery in a few weeks, she reported. I am confident that she will be all right, since her vision has been pinpointed like a laser beam on God for nearly thirty years. What makes her beliefs so interesting is that although she has a strongly focused spiritual life, she has never denied her humanity. She is a real breathing, arguing, smoking, shopping, tender, fallible woman.

July 18, 1992

This afternoon the temperature hit 112 degrees while Sasha and I were at the library to hear storyteller Joe Hayes. Afterward, when we reached the pavement, Sasha nearly keeled over and had to be carried to the car, where she whimpered until the air conditioner had worked its alchemy.

Any time the temperature inches over 110 degrees, I go crazy, too. I feel trapped while in the house, sick at the thought of going anywhere in the car, and horrified by the searing asphalt of parking lots. Sometimes it's even too hot to go outside and jump in the pool. This heat makes me want to run away.

My office was just graced by Sasha, a cloud of blonde hair and dreamy blue eyes. In her arms she had a white mechanical rabbit. "I love my rabbit big as the sky," she said. " I named it Cactus Tree." These confidences make mothering worth everything. Sasha and I are friends—a legacy left to me by my mother, who was not especially close to her mother or to other women. Nevertheless, she was able to forge a deep bond with me.

Cactus Tree is now hopping across my office floor to the dismay of Brujo, the big male shepherd, who would like to destroy it. Brujo cannot see the good of mechanical objects and often feels he must protect us from them, which is how he behaves with the vacuum, ripping into it as if it were attacking me. We will have to guard Cactus Tree carefully to avoid a terrible scene and bad feelings between Sasha and Brujo, whom she calls her brother.

July 19, 1992

The seven year old came for a lesson yesterday. As she was painting, I thumbed through the thirty black-and-white sketches in my little black drawing book, then began working them over with colors. While watching the hues flow back into my life, I wondered why the large paintings I've completed over the past three years are richly shaded whereas my private book is drained of color. The drawings are simple, strong, and replete with everything needed to turn them into big, intense paintings, but for some reason they came out one after another in black ink and stayed that way.

Not all the drawings were improved by the addition of color. Nevertheless, the little artist girl in me watercolored one after another with pleasure, thinking, "Here, Mommy. Look how happy I am!"

In creativity, as in life itself, one needs a wise inner parent. For me that wise woman is constantly providing direction, encouragement, and praise: "Go ahead! Put the paint on your drawings. It feels good, doesn't it? You've missed that. Let the colors run off your brush into the perfect spaces you created. They have been waiting for you."

I've spent much of my life looking for strong women to learn from. I wanted to know how they spoke, how they held themselves, where their dignity came from. I also wanted to know what they knew and where their radiance came from. After forty years, I have become the woman I was searching for all that time—a feat I attribute to the extraordinary teachers and guides who were placed on my path and were willing to be real.

Many role models in our society are actresses, entertainers, and models. But I could never understand the deification of women safely splayed out on two-dimensional planes in movie theaters or magazines. Airbrushed people, for some reason, did not radiate qualities I could aspire to. Instead, the women who influenced me were artists, art teachers, dancers, and therapists. Dorothy Royer, my first art teacher, glowed with a radiance I had rarely seen in other people, and became a prototype for my later spiritual mothers, all of whom were twenty or thirty years older than I. They were unpretentious women, often barefoot and in jeans, who listened to classical music or jazz. They were gardeners who grew herbs and drank strange teas. They were great cooks, never measuring or even following printed recipes.

These women were free spirits who did not live or think within the bounds of convention. Each one was attuned to the realms of dreams and feelings; had been in some form of therapy; was expressive, and encouraged self-expression in others. As a result, you could say anything to them. Listening deeply, they saved the sanity of those of us who did not conform to preferred modes of learning or being.

Of all the strong women I knew, the first was my mother, a wonderful eccentric with a big heart and a black sense of humor who was easily moved to tears and laughter. Life later gifted me with numerous brave women who chose to be themselves in a world that valued appearance at any cost. They gave me places to go when I needed help and support; they gave me solutions; their eyes were clear, and their reactions reliable. They lived lives I admired, and remarkably, they invited me into them.

These friendships set the stage for my relationship with Jeanne, a pioneer in the recovery movement who worked with young people and addicts, amid tremendous pressure to drop us on our faces. She was somewhat different from my other mentors—her personality was stronger, and she was more vocal. Like the others, however, she spoke the truth no matter what. She also had a big heart, a weird and twisted sense of humor, and an unwillingness to hide who she was. Jeanne is the one who informed me of the source of the radiance I had seen: "It's God, honey. Anything you see about me that you like I got from God." She had answers, and her answers worked.

July 20, 1992

I am waiting for a friend to visit. The dogs are draped around the office floor, and out my window roadrunners are crisscrossing the desert, their reptilian eyes glancing skeptically in the direction of the noises from my keyboard. Over the past few months this friend, like many others, has asked questions about my first book: "Why did you call it *Warrior Woman?* What *is* a warrior woman?"

The name, I explain, comes from a Hopi kachina. According to legend, she was a young woman working in the fields when her village was attacked by enemies. She took up weapons and courageously fought off the invaders until help arrived. Several years ago I painted a life-size picture of this figure, whereupon her presence became so strong in my life that I called the painting "Self-Portrait in Transition" and named my book after her. Although the name Warrior Woman burned itself into my soul, for me her path has nothing to do with going to war. Rather, it has to do with learning, growing, looking for truth, peeling away layers of distortion, and becoming who one really is despite great pressure to do otherwise.

Being a warrior woman is about following the inner voice, often in the face of tremendous fear. It's about letting inner radiance shine regardless of your surroundings and circumstances. And it's about giving others permission to do the same. The way of a warrior woman is a way of life for all women who walk at my side, including those who went before me and those who have yet to traverse the path through the forest.

July 21, 1992

It's 1:30 A.M. and I was recently awakened by the sounds of Puma gaily pouncing on an apparently lively prey. After a few minutes of listening to what seemed like sexual thrashings emanating from the bathroom, I had to pee regardless of what was going on in there. I also wanted to remove the new bathroom rug, to spare it from the little "art thing" Puma likes to do with entrails. So I rolled out of bed, stepped into the bathroom, and snatched up the rug, trying not to look at what he was doing.

He left his work momentarily to rub up against my leg, whereupon I made the mistake of glancing down. There I saw a rather sizable bushy-tailed pack rat looking up at me as if to say, "Don't tell your damn cat I'm not really dead." Involuntarily, I leaped and, turning, landed with amazing grace on the counter beside the sink. I don't mind rats per se; I simply did not want to get between Puma and his kill, because when I do, he thinks I want to play with them and proceeds to let the little creatures go free before my unbelieving eyes. We already have quite a rodent herd in the hacienda as a result of my failure to grasp the finer points of cat etiquette.

From my perch on the counter, I heard a sleepy "What is it?" Never one to withhold the truth from my husband, I answered, "A good-sized pack rat." And so the game of rat hockey began. Bob scored eight points for capturing the creature and ejecting it from the bedroom arena.

When played naked, this is a crowd-pleasing sport of beauty and splendor as participants fly through the air doing arabesques, jetés, and "moon shots." Players lose points for turning on lights, and fractions of points for unsportsmanlike conduct such as cat abuse or kicking. Bob, a ferocious gladiatorlike player, has had to learn some of the subtle nuances of the game—like not shooing away the cat or throwing him over the wall to the desert, since the cat is the best indicator of the rat's whereabouts, saving hours of guesswork.

When the fun ended, we plowed back into bed, but thoughts began churning in my head about a three-hour presentation on creativity I am scheduled to give at a recovery conference in Phoenix on Saturday. Soon I was running a slide show behind my closed eyes, previewing the opening to my talk. Never before had I shown slides, so I also began mentally projecting the images, discussing each one while sweating profusely.

Now I am out of bed and ready to strategize. Tomorrow I'll set up the light table and review my slides. Because Namka has warned me that projector bulbs often burn out during important slide presentations, I will take along an extra one, as well as a box of matches for making a tiny slide show if all else fails. In the event that things will go terribly awry, I'll also take some rags and gasoline.

I'm scared about speaking for long segments of time. In the past I thought that the more experience I had, the more this fear would subside, but that has not happened. Maybe it's time to act as if I love public presentations—which I do when they are over. Writing about my apprehensions feels more satisfying than turning them over in my mind . . .

I just floated out to the kitchen for a cup of tea with mesquite honey. On my return, while scanning the walls for giant cockroaches, it struck me that all I want to do is write, that nothing else will satisfy me. Although writing eats me up, interferes with my sleep, and has me inspecting the walls for nocturnal pests, I can't stop doing it. Most writers I've known worry that they won't be able to practice their craft; my concern is that I won't be able to *stop*.

When I write, I become like a transparent static-filled sock; everything in me empties out. In this sense, writing is similar to throwing up—once you start, some reflex takes over and you keep going until you seem to turn inside out. In another sense, writing is more gratifying than spewing forth the contents of your stomach, because there's always the possibility of fan mail to let you know that what you've done is changing people's lives. Just don't be fooled into thinking that a life of leisure awaits you, since it's unlikely that you'll be lazing around in your hammock waiting for large checks to arrive in your mailbox.

Chapter 11

She Dreams the Corn

Tucson, Arizona
July 23, 1992

The rains are here. Two days ago Bob and I set off on a hike with Sasha. Soon after we headed up the road in a gentle rain, the sky opened wide and dumped on us—much to our delight.

Yesterday's storm was even more compelling. During Jeff's lesson, rain slipping in through the roof fell onto the whirling overhead fans and spattered all over his drawings. How he achieved the wetness and the primitive circular movement of these pieces was beyond me until I discovered that the effects were taking place without his participation. How lovely it was to see the medium of rain at work!

The downpours have been pleasing to the birds as well. Out the window I see a thrasher poking delicate holes in the dark red fruit of a prickly pear and, as though they were the eyeballs of Prometheus, pulling out their flaming, wet innards with its long, curved beak. Meanwhile, a small convention of cactus wrens is happily picking at lint and strings that have become caught on a high branch of cholla. In the palo verde another wren is waging a holy war to pull off a cluster of stubborn leaves. She is getting mad, hopping up and down with no dignity whatsoever. Cactus wrens are little coyotes with wings, and I have come to love them.

As the days go by, I am growing increasingly more restless, eager to set out for Santa Fe. When you know what you want to do, it's a superhuman feat to hold still and wait for life to take you there.

July 28, 1992

I've just returned from the dreaded presentation in Phoenix which, as it turned out, went well, even though the audience was packed with far more people than I expected. Showing slides of the paintings proved to be a good idea. The crowd was receptive and the time went by quickly.

Today time is not going by quickly, for I have received news that Jeanne is back in the hospital due to complications from the surgery. I am lost in a "feeling memory," reflecting on my years of depression and despair before she and I crossed paths. I remember sitting in various residences in France, Switzerland, and England, hung over and horrified at what I had done the night before. I was ensconced in a life that had no apparent way out other than through death. And although I was certainly doing my part, death eluded me; degradation, however, did not.

While looking for a 12-step meeting in Los Angeles upon my return, I ran across Jeanne at a water fountain in Roxbury Park. She knew in an instant that I was dying; and because of her knowing, my life began. No one else recognized the extent of my despair and self-hatred. God had delivered me into the hands of a most extraordinary woman!

At meetings, people often said to Jeanne, "How wonderful that she is getting help at such a young age," whereupon Jeanne would reply, "Tina isn't young. She has come with death as a companion." In the months that followed I realized that although I sought help and did the work—plenty of it—it was Jeanne's ability to see who I was and what I had become that enabled me to tolerate the company of human beings. It took an army to keep me from dropping into hell, yet I always knew she was there in the background watching over me, praying her strong prayers.

I used to dream of Jeanne walking down dark hallways while holding a match in front of me. Now the haunting question is, what will happen after she has gone? Closing my eyes, I can see all the women I have loved these last seventeen years forming a huge web that will catch me. Under their kitchen sinks all of them together have enough containers to collect my tears. Real healing, after all, requires not only that I help them but that when it is my time to grow, they are there to watch over me, pray, hold me, and give me their love. They will be there with their small earthen jars waiting to catch the rain when it starts.

A young coyote is passing through the cactus forest outside my window. She is a ghost dog, nearly transparent in her desert dress. How like a dream it is to see her calmly wandering through the mesquite and prickly pear—a wild sister come to call.

July 30, 1992

I have been working steadily to prepare the house for sale. When it is ready, strange people will come poking through my safe haven wondering why I have skeletons hanging in my closet. I'm sure that Heidi, who will be handling the transactions, won't ask me to take them down—maybe the shrunken heads, but not the skeletons.

Yesterday I brought out an old twenty-four-by-thirty-inch gessoed canvas and began a painting—not out of desire, but simply because I have many lessons coming up. The reason I had no yearning to start another painting was that plunging in might only delay my departure. If I continue to act like I live here, I reasoned, God may forget to move me.

The painting I started was inspired by an image in my black book of a woman sleeping in the desert amid ears of corn in many colors. The central figure—She Dreams the Corn—is the solitary being in me who felt compelled to come into the desert to live. Not only is she enraptured by this landscape but it is the source of her disturbing and compelling dreams. Here in the wastelands, her fertility and inventiveness know no bounds, and flowers sprout out of her head.

July 31, 1992

It's 5:30 A.M. and I am gazing out my open window enjoying one of the few cool moments of the day. I can feel the presence of Coyote Woman dancing around me in a circle just out of the reach of light. I can smell her, too. She's prancing, with ears pricked and a sometimes canine, sometimes human grin. And she's laughing like a lunatic.

Tomorrow I will be attending a Women's Day circle of seventy-five participants—a special ritual for indomitable women of the desert who wander the mountains and canyons. Tomorrow we dance.

The next day I will be visiting Jeanne. It's odd that I've never felt judged by her. Not once in the early days of our relationship did she act superior to my sniveling, wormlike being. Although she did appear shocked when I was about to walk out of my first marriage, she was not bowled over by my revelations, which I now know resembled the secret thoughts of a four and a half year old; she even held me as I squeezed out embarrassing confessions of jealousy toward her. Nor did she laugh at me, though she certainly made me laugh.

Jeanne will be here a long time, I trust. Nevertheless, she has begun the process of letting go of some of her earthly ties. Although I don't understand it, I can feel it moving me along like the wind. It's not a question of choice; it's a matter of survival. Along with these thoughts come practical considerations. It was Jeanne who first gave me a membership in the Hemlock Society, the organization that opened the door when it was time for my mother to go. I, too, am an avid supporter of an individual's right to die—my mother's, Jeanne's, and mine as well.

As for me, I have a living will and do not wish to be kept alive by ridiculous and costly means if there is no prospect of recovery. When it is time for me to go, I'm going. If I'm in pain, give me morphine—with all the syringes you've got. Don't force me to hang around ruining the joy and hope in my daughter's sparkling eyes.

Coming away from the concrete of Los Angeles and seeing the desert in the mornings has changed my life forever.

Pecos, New Mexico
August 11, 1992

Things are moving so fast that I become bogged down any time I try to verbalize my experiences. The Women's Day ritual was both powerful and deeply gratifying. My subsequent visit with Jeanne, although brief, was reassuring. I needed to look in her eyes and put my arms around her. Although she isn't herself yet, her spirit is intact.

Upon my return to Tucson, I lugged my older paintings out of the barn and propped them up against mesquite trees for a little exhibit. Hot and sweaty, I was dressed in my Guatemalan shorts and pink rubber thongs—not quite gallery-type attire. But even so, some paintings sold. Heidi bought three, and other friends gave good homes to many more. We sat in the shade of the trees and made our deals. They were happy; I was happy.

Now I am alongside the Pecos River for another recharging dose of New Mexico. Bob, Sasha, and I are staying with our friends Susan and Lee. Susan—originally Sue, from New York—is joyously living the life of a cowgirl. She's been doing ranch chores and running errands with dead antelopes since we arrived, so we've had the place pretty much to ourselves.

The air is cool, and a stillness buttons down around the cozy ranch house as night unfolds. Last night I had the luxury of sleeping beside Bob, with no child between us. He is warm like a bear when we fall asleep.

August 12, 1992

This afternoon Sasha and I headed up the lane to the main road. As we rounded the bend, we came to a thick stand of tall trees. For a moment I felt like I was back at my parents' spread at Hat Creek, where time seemed to stand still and all that mattered were the leaves on the trees, the wind, the stars, and an occasional blue heron. At the time, I was sure my parents would always be there, growing into crusty old mountain people in a forest that would eventually become too dense for me to penetrate.

I wept to think that Sasha would never experience the pleasures of that isolated place, and that my parents would never see my little girl stomping down country roads and up the sides of mountains ever more steep, keeping pace with me as I stride along. At that moment, a blonde moppet came up alongside me with one of those puffy white dandelion balls you blow on to make wishes. "Here, Mama. You wanted this, didn't you?" Yes, I thought. "You wanted it, but you wanted me to get it for you, didn't you?" Right again. Seeing the blood of my tribe beating in her veins, I knew that love endures.

"Let's be coyotes, Mama, okay?" she proposed. We began to howl loudly, whereupon Beau, Susan's bluetick hound, started baying in a nearby field. My howl had a keening edge to it, whereas Sasha's was filled with joy at being alive.

Santa Fe, New Mexico
August 13, 1992

Here we are at Dan and Ruby's house in Santa Fe, where it's been raining in the afternoons. This afternoon, however, the sky is crystalline and the piñon freshly green. Such shifts in nature pull at my heart.

This sinking into the senses gives the illusion of a lengthening of time, and elongated moments of beauty are what draw me back to Santa Fe. Today I am being reimprinted with the colors and textures of my life.

We are not yet looking for a house here, or ready to tackle all the details of moving. Still, although Tucson was the right place to help my mother leave this plane of existence, I long to stay in Santa Fe. I want to go on with the part of my life that has been quietly continuing here, waiting for me to remember that this is where I belong.

Tucson, Arizona
August 16, 1992

I hope the family sleeps in, since I'm burning to write—a passion that often occurs when I'm letting go for the unknown. My dreams last night were frightening, probably because I'm afraid I won't find a house I love in Santa Fe. The answer, I know, is that I won't have to, that my home is in the process of finding *me*. Still, each time I go through these cycles of massive change, I worry that I won't find a suitable cave—tribal vestiges, I'm sure. My instincts never rest until the place has been found, and this time the urgency is magnified, for winter is waiting in the wings.

More revelations emerged last night during a signing for *Warrior Woman* at a bookstore here in Tucson. The people who came asked me to read from the book, which I was happy to do. I enjoyed listening to their laughs and comments as I read about my departure from Los Angeles. While writing these passages, I suddenly realized, I had no idea that six years later I would be married to Bob Earll, who appears in several segments of the book; I would have a daughter; both my parents would be dead; and I would be speaking publicly about writing and making art. No way was there to know that such twists and turns were awaiting me on my path.

Reading made the time pass meaningfully. It comforted me, especially the portions describing my experience of impending change. It also validated the existence of forces larger than my will that occasionally take over. Unseen forces guide my life, I concluded, and my choice is to surrender to them or to balk at them until the bulldozer rolls over me. God, give me patience while I'm on hold. I'm beating myself to death from the inside out.

August 17, 1992

Bleary-eyed, I am listening to music and watching colors slowly bleed back into the world. They all disappeared the moment I woke up with Sasha's feet in my face as she was trying to wedge one of them into my mouth. Does every child sleep backward in bed or is mine somehow bent?

While my eyes readjust, I am incubating images for a new series of paintings. Taking my old work out of the barn last week reminded me of how hard it would be to replicate these early paintings of weird people, because I don't hate people the way I used to. When I first entered therapy, I found it cathartic to paint individuals the way I saw them, since they frightened me. To outsiders the canvases look like clips from a Fellini movie, but to me they are reminiscent of the alienation I was feeling and the relief I experienced when they were finished.

My current desire is to paint the outrageous-looking people of Santa Fe. There dressing up is an art form, as it is a city of strong individuals with few inhibitions or social pressures guiding styles of dress. Sitting at the fountain across from Pasqual's, I will surely find enough material for years of painting. I also want to make drawings of people "in costume" on the Plaza. Oh, it's a field day in that town for weird humans, especially when the tourists start to appear! If I sketch and then paint the town's people, maybe I'll be able to hold onto a little of Santa Fe when I return to exile. New Mexico has a hold on me just as the desert did when all I could think of were the rocks, outcroppings where rattlers napped at noon, spring flowers, and the seductive mystery of this forbidding land.

August 18, 1992

I awoke thinking of how to wrap up the work with my students. Tonight, for example, a group of women will be coming for a concluding workshop on creativity and cycles of the moon. I'll most likely tell them that when I'm on a creative binge, I rely on phases of the moon for extra energy and structure. The time for starting big projects such as large paintings, I've found, is when the new moon begins, for then we can take advantage of the increasing tension she evokes as she comes into her fullness. The time following the full moon is best for completing projects, for tying up those flapping loose ends.

The format of the workshop is outlining itself nicely on the yellow legal pad I keep on my worktable. The two and a half hours will pass quickly, as they usually do when my students bear down and I serve as the midwife.

Yesterday Jeanne and I spoke at length about my move to Santa Fe. Up till then I had been soft-pedaling my intense need to return, editing my words to sound as if relocating were not an inner imperative but rather a remote possibility. I didn't want her to think I was moving farther away from her. Our most recent conversation, however, set me free.

Jeanne's feedback came in variations on the "You can't go home again" theme. "You may not be able to capture the feelings you had there before," she cautioned, "although you may find new, equally wonderful feelings. New Mexico will never be the same; it can't be." Her words had a ring of truth to them, and also a tone of sadness. She knows I have to go.

August 22, 1992

The latter part of this week has been horrific. Four days ago Sasha fell from her new bunk bed. Hearing the thump, I ran to her room and found her prone on the floor. After struggling to calm myself, I attempted to assess the damage and found that the wind had been knocked out of her. When I asked her to walk, she took one shaky step and fell, at which point Bob decided she should be seen in the emergency room. I held her in my arms as my ex-ambulance driver–husband raced us to the hospital. "I'm tired, Mama. I'm going to sleep," Sasha said as we careened around a corner. "Wake up, honey, and talk to Mama," I urged. "Where does it hurt?" Immediately, her eyes rolled back in her head. Soon afterward, she threw up on me. Each passing moment we thought might be her last.

At the hospital, I jumped from the car and dashed inside with Sasha still in my arms. The nurse at the front desk was on the phone reading from a sheet of paper and gesticulating, all the while looking the other way. A deep sob escaped from me. "She's fallen," I choked out. Everything stopped, and we were rushed into an examining room, where Sasha was hooked up to monitors as she continued to drift in and out of consciousness. Bob and I, meanwhile, were in another world tracking her small spirit, looking for her, clinging to her. We pleaded, "Stay, Alexandra. Stay with us." We prayed, "It's your child, God, but please send her back to us."

A moment later Sasha was whisked off for a brain scan, and we followed. There we stood in heavy aprons while the machine droned on, probing the secrets of our child's brain. After the test, she leaned over and vomited blood. We were undone, sure that she was slipping from our lives. "No," the nurse assured us, "she has a bloody nose from the impact, and the blood has gone into her throat."

At long last, the results of the scan were revealed: "She has a fractured skull. Lots of possibilities, lots of unknowns . . . They're usually all right . . . She'll have to be admitted and observed overnight." Bob and I made camp on the pediatrics ward. As the hours passed, we held Sasha's tiny hands and noticed that although she slept nearly nonstop, she could be roused. Convinced that her grandmother was in the realms Sasha was cruising, I begged, "Send her back, Didi."

In the three days that have elapsed since Sasha's crash, she has steadily improved. This morning she appeared in the kitchen wearing a skirt with pink stripes that went one way and a shirt with green stripes that went another. Layered beneath the green stripes was a T-shirt emblazoned with "Poco Loco Club" in big black letters. She had pushed her blonde mop up from her forehead and secured it with a large red-and-white bow. "I'm not sick anymore. I flew, Mama," she announced.

I was visibly relieved, having spent days and nights acutely aware that a child is the most precious being a woman can ever have in her life, but what pain—and love—this opens us to. Children worm their way much farther into a life than we adults can with our clumsy wiles and barbed-wire caresses. Children dance their way into our souls. And when their bright and clear gaze, clean laughter, and sweet little kisses are in any way endangered, reality swiftly zooms into perspective and we see that nothing else matters!

Now that life has returned to some semblance of normal, I've begun rescheduling this week's classes into next week. When I called Jane, who is now in her fifth month of art lessons and is beginning to come to life after her divorce, she said she wanted the "painting of the woman who is filling the earth around her with the corn she is dreaming in so many colors." Corn Woman belongs with someone who works from her unconscious and is awakening to herself; knowing that Jane will have her is therefore thrilling and will bring me great pleasure as I finish the painting.

August 24, 1992

Last night I dreamed of a group discussion about a piece of my artwork. The piece was gold and red, and portrayed three horses, one of which was large, as well as rattlesnakes coiled here and there. I couldn't see it until I'd begun presenting it to the group. Although Bob was pressing me to hurry, I managed to explain, "The horses are my feelings, uncontrollable feelings coming up to the surface and breaking out. The snake people know everything—the slightest vibrations and whispered secrets of this world as well as the other one."

Janee is coming for a lesson today. I'm looking forward to seeing her, and I'm also eager to paint. I haven't picked up my paints since the family's last trip to Santa Fe, more than ten days ago. She Who Dreams the Corn is on the easel waiting for me to come finish her.

September 3, 1992

Inspired by the delivery of Janee's astounding quilt, which may well hang in a museum one day, I took Sasha to a quilt show at Tohono Chul Park. It was meltingly hot as we approached the doorway of one of the most enchanting places in Tucson. Once inside, I began craning my neck to decide where to start when I heard a small voice at my side, saying, "Mama, it's too hot." I looked down to see my free-spirited daughter wearing nothing but her Little Mermaid underpants and her new red cowgirl boots, and waving her dress through the air to "cool it off."

Janee's quilt, titled "If the Amish Were Navajos," is exquisite to behold. Richly colored in turquoise, purple, and purple paisley, with a bold red lick here and there—all on a black field—the design has a spin to it due to the way she pieced the blocks. How amazing that this treasure is the result of a trade for art lessons! Little did I know during our negotiations that I would become the recipient of what is surely one of the most beautiful quilts in existence.

September 7, 1992

Yesterday, on the first anniversary of my mother's death, we held an "estate sale" to clear out the old and make way for the new. Our two-car garage was crammed to the gills like some wonderful junk shop. Heidi, a veteran garage-sale maven, helped with the pricing, and Deb, another friend, pitched in on the arranging and tagging. In addition to furniture and odds and ends, we sold about twenty-five paintings and twenty etchings. It was one of the best parties I ever threw.

Marti, an extraordinary masseuse, came to pick out paintings, and enthusiastically pulled out everything she liked after I told her I would be overjoyed to receive massages in payment. The real gift for me was the happiness she exuded at the prospect of having all the paintings she wanted.

Marti just lost her father, with whom she was very close, so I felt comfortable reminding her that my mom died one year ago. Marti had been involved in the final caregiving, providing my mother with luxurious foot rubs and back rubs, and forming part of the circle of love that closed around her in her last days. My mother welcomed Marti to her bedside, which at the time helped me see that when some people die, the universe pulls the best folks in around them to form a protective cocoon.

Reflecting on our losses, Marti and I wept together amid the goings-on in my garage. Between sobs, I told her of a terrible experience I'd had the night before, on the anniversary of the final stages of the deathwatch, feeling alternately feverish and chilled; waking up and being unable to go back to sleep; tossing, turning, and fretting. It was a great release to cry with another woman who had lost a treasured parent.

Also at the sale was a woman I'd never met before, who arrived with her nine-year-old daughter. Right away the girl asked me whose house this was. "Mine . . . now," I replied, suddenly aware that her mother had prepared her for attending an estate sale, which meant that someone in the family had died. After we traded little pieces of information, the woman remarked that her mother, too, had died. "How long does it hurt this bad?" I asked. "For me it took about a year and a half before the terrible pain went. After that, it gradually got much better. You still miss them, but without the anguish," she confided. "I needed to know that," I told her. "You must have been sent by God today." She admitted that she had no idea why she came, that she had felt drawn to be here.

I am experiencing considerable ambivalence about leaving the warm, open people of Tucson. Yet I know Santa Fe is a good place for me as an artist. I console myself with fantasies of a home in both places.

Chapter 12

Cloud Woman

Santa Fe, New Mexico
September 16, 1992

Today I am forty-one years old, and we have returned to Dan and Ruby's house in Santa Fe to celebrate, although I hardly feel celebratory. I woke up knowing I was not going to receive a birthday present; then Bob woke up, and we had a fight that finished me off. Retreating to Ruby's bedroom, I knew the minute she put her arms around me that I needed to cry. Women understand that emotional storms roll in on birthdays.

I am a child about my birthday. I like to have a little fuss made over me. And now that the people who once upon a time made the biggest fuss are gone, I need festivity.

As it turned out, my birthday went quite well. After a good cry and some protracted whining, I did a little writing and fell into a deep well of grief for my mother. Then our longtime friend Jim came to take me house hunting, and I crumpled into his arms sobbing. I don't have to pretend around him.

After that, the day brightened. My mother did not come back from the other side with a gift; nor did Bob and I get away from the kid long enough to make mad, passionate love. But we did stop fighting, and I did pick out a present. By the time I was seated at a lovely dinner, everything was just ducky.

Tucson, Arizona
September 19, 1992

I've been trying to phone my sister's daughter, Kris, in Sardinia to wish her a happy birthday, but I'm having a hard time getting through. Sasha calls her Aunt Kiss. Kris, who at the age of seventeen lost her mom, has paid her dues and been promoted from cousin to aunt. Sasha needed an aunt.

It is pleasing to have family living in Italy. Against the odds, Sharon's daughter has made a good life there with a husband and a beautiful son. Once ravaged by drugs and alcohol, our formerly doomed clan is coming back to life.

And so is my desire to paint. During our long drive across the desert from New Mexico, a scene in the rearview mirror caught my eye: my face, set against an unimaginably blue sky, was reflected in a very soft focus, and the voluminous white clouds of New Mexico were superimposed across my forehead like a *tablita,* a headdress worn by Pueblo women dancers. As I watched, a mask subtly dropped over my face, and I saw instead the face of Cloud Woman—someone new.

Since the transition to my next life is taking much longer than anticipated, I am thinking of painting Cloud Woman. These past few days I have been drawing her in oil pastels in my sketchbook.

September 22, 1992

The beauty of my surroundings is captivating. I am still amused by the sight of cactus wrens pulling threads from the cholla for their nests. I am touched, too, by the sight of these tiny red-throated birds eating from the fruit of the cow's tongue cactus, their delicate feet clinging to the pads and their small throats stained even redder with the juice of the fruit. Looking out onto this "private game reserve," I realize that a portion of my heart and spirit will always remain here in this room that has become my refuge.

Simultaneously, I am absorbed by the thought of painting on my easel in Santa Fe. Oh, the ripping and tearing will be hard on the heart when the moving van pulls out of here, and I will miss my Tucson friends, but the time is approaching for me to go.

In the interim, despite a distinct lack of drive, I plan to start the painting of Cloud Woman—a woman of the sky who is likely to free me from feelings of bondage. I know paintings can do this, because "Wind Spirits over the Desert," which I started before Sasha was born, placated the part of me that envisioned being shackled to the nursery following her arrival. That painting calmed the wild horses in me that were fearful of being corralled.

This afternoon I'm planning to visit the Arizona School for the Deaf and Blind. Marilyn Draving, who came to one of my workshops, teaches a class there in plaster face-casting, and invited me to come so her students could make a mask of my face.

September 28, 1992

My impatience grows with each passing day. I pace; clean out drawers, cupboards, closets; sell a painting or two. At night I sometimes dream of moving the final remnants of my belongings from the house I grew up in.

The visit to Marilyn's class was a wondrous adventure. Six kids who can hear well but see only with their hearts came into the room and introduced themselves with a handshake, standing up close to me and saying exactly what was on their minds. After draping me with a sheet and tying back my hair, they put on classical music and told me to think of things I liked. Then they spread wet strips of plaster across my face, touching me with fingers that were more perceptive than any I have known.

The kids often asked how I was doing, and although I could not talk through the plaster, I could croak and moan and even squeak out a diabolical laugh without moving my mouth. As I lost the use of my eyes, the kids' personalities grew more and more pronounced. While four students thoughtfully pressed plaster gauze into the corners of my eye sockets and around the curves of my nostrils, Manny massaged my shoulders and Andrea served as my guide.

Andrea was the artist-writer of the bunch. She had the most complex communication skills, a capacity to ask thought-provoking questions, and an uncanny ability to decipher the answers. The others were also communicative and able to reach into human beings, each in their own way. I could tell that Marilyn had been working respectfully with them and boosting their confidence. Clearly, they were learning much more than plaster face-casting.

At the end of our session, Marilyn said, "Let's sit down and ask Tina some questions about her life. Tina's an artist and she's written a book. How many people here like art?" Without a moment's hesitation, every hand in the room shot up. Then the questions began, and as I answered them, I sculpted my words. The kids, in turn, took them in with profound intensity and concentration. Seemingly listening with their nerve endings, they brought the words down into themselves, sorting, sifting, and weighing the meanings in every part of their being. Each one of them said they loved music, and I could see they truly did.

October 14, 1992

I am tapping away before dawn. A few minutes ago the giant palo verde tree outside my office woke me up announcing in a frightened voice that palo verde beetles, wicked-looking prehistoric predators, were killing her. Her words were filled with urgency: "Tina, wake up! I will die if you do not stop them quickly."

At church on Sunday, Bob and I ran into Hugh and Gayle, friends who used to live in Santa Fe, and together we slipped off for a salad after the service. They told us they spent years moving from place to place. Such an adventurous lifestyle, they explained, is both a blessing and a curse. I was relieved to have found like-minded souls who, like us, are called hither and yon by unseen impulses. One more move, however, and I hope to become rooted, because farther down the road Sasha will be forming long-term attachments—delicate emotional threads that are subject to breaking with each departure.

In the midst of all this churning, I have been painting the edges of all the large works I created here. I wonder if I will ever again paint pieces that astonish me.

November 1, 1992

New Mexico feels as far away as Thailand. I want to believe that the universe is working out the details of our move, that a better place is being prepared for us, but on a scale of one to ten, my discomfort is registering at eight. I am plagued by an ever-present feeling of being in the wrong place. Even so, I am able to enjoy being with my students, to fulfill my commitments, and to see the beauty and harmony around me.

I wonder what else besides my life in Tucson is coming to a close. Paintings, sketches, and relationships, too, start up and end in their own time. All I get to do is grab some clothes, pack my bag, and try to keep my shoelaces tied.

A new me is forming. Although it is only a tiny seed of what it will become, I am flooded with excitement. If prospects feel this good now, what might emerge from the new and improved rendition? Surely, I will fly across the evening sky on a wild horse, shooting golden sparks all around me.

November 2, 1992
Day of the Dead

I'm missing my mother more than usual this morning. On my desk is a photograph of her kissing Sasha on her first day of school. How perfectly it captures the outpouring of love and understanding that streamed from grandmother to granddaughter!

My mother was rarely this demonstrative, however. Having been shoved into the life of a child actress, she had been forced to show affection to legions of people she detested, so she knew better than to expect the same of another child. She never pressured her granddaughter to kiss her or sit on her lap or be physically affectionate; all such actions had to originate with Sasha. This approach took much restraint on Mom's part, because she was kid-crazy. Cleverly, she figured out all sorts of ways to get next to Sasha, like building pillow forts on her bed and taking her out to the local coffee shop, where they'd sit side by side in a booth. Mom was an artist about giving kids an illusion of freedom, and as a result of her deftness, whenever Sasha had a problem with Bob or me, she knew exactly where to find an ally.

Jane, who now has "Woman Dreaming the Corn" in her house, is coming to paint tomorrow. While she's at the easel, I'll be starting a raw and beautiful painting of a mask I sketched of myself while in Mexico. In the oil-pastel sketch, I have feathers coming out of my head, a lightning bolt running down my cheek, and red teardrops splattered on my black dress. This otherworldly figure is a direct descendant of "Self-Portrait in Transition," on the cover of *Warrior Woman*. Whereas that image evokes terror and awe, and vibrates off the canvas, the new power-mask self-portrait will be more strengthening and challenging.

November 6, 1992

I have been working on the power-mask painting for the last few days. Actually, *it* has been working on *me*. This formidable piece challenges me to portray the eyes as searing as I see them in my mind.

I pause often while working on it. In fact, I'm pausing more in general these days, wondering about the delay in our return to Santa Fe. I frequently remind myself to hold still and grow up. Holding still in spite of my restlessness has forced me into an altered state. Seeing and hearing are sharpened considerably by desperation.

The power-mask image represents a landmark in my growth as a painter and a woman. Like the little pencil scratches my mother etched on the wall to mark my height, this painting suggests that a major growth spurt has taken place. I have come back from the Land of the Dead, and all the extraneous debris has been burned away. I'm not dancing yet, but I *am* upright.

The palo verde tree, having received an antidote against the infestation of palo verde beetles, is also in a state of repair. Although she has lost a large branch, I think she will live.

November 9, 1992

We're two days away from a full moon. Marking my life in this way may be a sign that I'm suffering from lunar dependency, or perhaps outright lunacy.

This morning Sasha used tape and paper to make a little book; she then drew "pictographs" on every page of it. She's been carrying this volume around and reading it for hours. At one point she told me she was going to write in her book every day. That's how I wrote mine, I thought to myself. Why is writing a book made out to be so much more complicated?

Another profundity recently rolled off Sasha's lips. As we rode along in the car, she was looking dreamily out into space when suddenly she said, "I'm going to miss me when I'm died. I'm really, really going to miss me."

November 15, 1992

Bob is out of town on business and Sasha is curled up on the bed in my office. Tired of trying to coax her to sleep in her room, I agreed to let her drift off here, provided that she remain quiet so I can work. She is peeking out at me from under her straw-colored haze of hair like a mischievous leprechaun. I'm pretending not to notice.

Earlier this evening, Sasha and I walked the hounds down the dirt road, as we often do at night. This time, however, the moment our eyes became accustomed to the dark, we tucked our flashlights in our pockets. (It's too cold this time of year to be concerned about rattlers.) As I watched the small hooded figure of my daughter running happily after the dogs, a wave of well-being washed over me. Drinking in the joy of my four-legged friends bounding into the chaparral, Sasha's exuberance, the cold eddies of air around my legs, and the desert sky aglow with stars, I said to myself, "Lucky me." Despite my proclivity for jumping into the abyss, my life has been full and rich.

Several days ago I started yet another painting of Coyote Woman. I hate it—which is strange, because I liked the preliminary drawing. Over and over again I've changed the colors, the style, the mood, but no matter what I do, I want to put my foot through the thing. It's too weak!

I am determined to come up with a great painting of Coyote Woman—an image that vibrates with coyote magic—if I have to paint her twenty times. She's vain; she wants to be painted. Yet each time I begin, I feel her close by, laughing at me.

For more than two years I've been tracking an elusive coyote bitch. On one canvas, I've painted her true to size and dancing; on another, soft and diffuse; but I have yet to capture her in her full power, crackling and luminous. One day she will emerge vibrant and charged with an energy that emanates from the studio into the house and out into the desert, flowing down the washes to places beyond the Southwest. The Coyote Woman I am after will flood the entire country with the energy of strong, changing women, and those who see her will know something of what I have experienced. That canvas will be more than a painting; it will be a ceremonial object.

November 16, 1992

I'm watching a four-inch-long rock squirrel feast on the old fruit of a barrel cactus. The critter is holding her little yellow prize in her front paws and suspiciously eyeing me at my desk. "It's okay," I want to say. "I'm a big squirrel with a computer."

Clarissa Pinkola Éstes's book *Women Who Run with the Wolves* has slowed me down. Not only do I savor these stories but I've made marks on almost every page I've read. Although I'm only a few chapters into the massive volume, already about thirty little yellow Post-its are sticking out to remind me of important passages. It has been years since I've been so engrossed in a book.

Inspired by Éstes, my sleep is now filled with dreams. I have placed a yellow legal pad next to my bed to catch them as they fly out. Like a woman who has lost her shadow, I've missed the dreamworld I once entered so reliably every night.

November 23, 1992

In last night's dream I was standing on a mesa top while a storm was threatening. From my left, a sharp-eyed hawk descended with deadly intent. I saw then that I was a supernatural being; my face was covered and my hair ceremonially prepared. My attacker, it turned out, was not a bird of prey, but rather a being sent by a well-respected leader of the village with whom I was engaged in a lifelong power struggle. I had not been a "good woman" in my tribe: I was considered insolent, too free, and not subservient enough, especially to this man.

Fighting for my life, I managed to fend off the attack, at which point I was required to find a new home. I subsequently moved some distance away, into a cave on the side of another mesa, where I lived for many years ostracized from my clan and steeped in loneliness. One day I was told that my former enemy was growing old, had no family, and needed someone to look after him. I went to him and stayed until it was his time to die, realizing too late that we cared for each other and always had.

Upon awakening, I identified the man as my husband in this lifetime, and the power struggle as one I have not been wise enough to stop. The dream has evidently emerged to help me break through the stubbornness and arrogance I'm exhibiting this time around. Such a breakthrough is not easy, and now I see it *never was.*

November 24, 1992

Another dream has come . . . I was trying to awaken my father, who was asleep on the couch in the house I grew up in. "Wake up! Mom's been gone all day with the car and the dog," I told him, intuitively aware that she had committed suicide. No sooner had I relaxed my vigilance over her than she managed to slip through my fingers, much to my dismay.

I tried to explain this situation to my dad, urging him to call the police yet simultaneously aware that she hadn't been missing long enough for us to file a report. I was worried sick about the young female dog, fearful that my mother had taken the creature into the ocean or off a winding road. Filled with grief and panic over having failed at my life's mission, I woke up weeping.

Now I am wondering about my great concern for the dog—who must represent an untamed aspect of myself. Has the part of me that relishes freedom and joy died with my mother? Watching most of my family die has left me unrecognizable. As people I love were ripped from my life, my creativity expanded, blown open by sadness; but the part of me that could let loose and fly—the dancer and prancer—is nowhere to be seen.

November 27, 1992

A third dream has surfaced . . . I was watching a game in a coliseum when people began parading by with various animals. One of the people was an attractive woman with long dark hair and a flowing white dress. "She is beautiful," I said to myself, and then noticed several small horses at her side. Immediately, one of them trotted over and began nuzzling me. "His name is Griffin," the woman explained. "Take care of him."

After about twenty minutes of enjoying the company of this affectionate creature, I walked off with Bob. Horrified to discover I had forgotten the small horse, I rushed back, only to find the beautiful woman leaving the building with him in her arms. Having both disappointed her and lost the tiny horse, I woke up distraught.

Over the past twenty years of tracking my dreams, I have had numerous encounters with the mystical horses that populate my inner world, representing the wildest, most emotional part of myself. This aspect of myself, I now see, is languishing from neglect. In the process of caretaking my mother, husband, child, and house, I have failed to see to my own hungers.

My first instinct is to lead with the intellect and assault myself with questions, such as "What caused this to happen?" and "Why have I lost my wild abandon?" Beneath this impulse, however, is a desire to take action—to passionately reclaim my life force. Once again, I will ride horses and sing and dance and make love under the stars.

November 28, 1992

These past five days I have been subjected to deeply disturbing tales from the interior. A small band of fighters surrounded by hostile forces is sounding a series of alarms. "I hear your calls for help," I tell them. "I'm coming down in a basket at the end of a long rope. Fight for your lives till I get there!"

I am on Mount Lemmon with the women from my Thursday night group, occupying the same cabin we rented last Thanksgiving weekend when, physically and emotionally depleted, I was glad my mother was dead, relieved that the ordeal was over. Janee was sitting by the fire sewing together the first squares of her quilt as the late afternoon light, filtering in through the window, ignited the turquoise, purple, paisley, and red. I watched, mesmerized, while she pieced and stitched, and I drew comfort from her neat and orderly threadwork.

This year I am missing my mother, father, sister—the whole beloved octopus. Furthermore, I am missing vital pieces of myself. I'm being called upon to reach into the swirling waters that urge me to paint and write. Now the message is: "Don't ask. Don't wait. Just do it."

Last night as I wrote at the kitchen table in our cabin, Mary Lou, from Phoenix, asked me what I was working on. "The next book," I told her. "You never stop, do you?" she replied. "Well, no. I keep count, and every two or three hundred pages I add a front and back cover. Once upon a time . . . the end. Many years later . . . meanwhile, back at the ranch. While writing, I tell my secrets, strewing the contents of my inner life across patiently listening pages. Sometimes I write and see paintings; other times I write about my paintings and more images appear."

December 7, 1992

Tomorrow we leave for Santa Fe. Bob cleverly thought up a reason for the excursion: to get work done on his car. I'm infinitely grateful, of course, although in recent months I have had little desire to return, since moving there seems out of reach. I don't like to drool over things I cannot have.

December 9, 1992

Yesterday we were ready to set off across the desert, but I woke up sick as a dog. Moreover, an end-of-the-world storm had hit the Southwest and rain was pelting down. While resting in bed later in the morning, I saw a coyote sniffing along the earthy ridge just a few yards from the bedroom door. Stepping quietly to the doorway to watch its peaceful progress, I saw its partner sauntering along a game trail about ten feet away. Spotting me, the coyote took a startled step backward, then decided to ignore me and follow its friend. I spent the day in bed.

This morning we made a bit more progress. After loading up the van, we traveled about forty-five miles east on I-40 when we noticed a coyote crossing the pavement up ahead. As soon as it it reached the center divide, it began to pace to and fro, nervously awaiting a chance to cross the westbound lanes. Within half an hour of that coyote sighting, Sasha told us her head hurt; she then complained of being sick to her stomach. Soon afterward, Bob was showing signs of weariness and said he might have a cold. Discouraged, we turned back.

By the time we hit Tucson, Sasha was fine and raring to go to school. Rummaging through the travel food we'd packed in the ice chest, I made her lunch. I am glad we have learned to be flexible, for in this state of flow magic can happen.

No sooner did Bob and I walk in the door than Heidi called to say that in a few hours a potential buyer would be coming to look at the house. But alas, no one showed up, and our hopes were dashed. Apparently, we are being asked to live in the present.

Tonight I took the dogs for a full-moon walk. Alternately wolfish, bearlike, and coyote-ish, these loyal companions were a joy to watch. Inspired by their nocturnal exuberance as well as by the desert around me as it began to melt into a silver soup, I settled upon a proper honoring for this cycle of change: a prayer about powerlessness and the need to stop fighting, hurrying, and worrying. While diving down into this prayer, I felt my edges merge with the chrome desert.

On our return to the hacienda, which was backlit, I stepped along the brick walkway painted silver by the moon. "I'm here for now," I said aloud. "The path is illuminated before me, and I'm here for this beautiful night. Beyond that, I know nothing."

December 13, 1992

The latest painting of Coyote Woman is finished, and I am pleased with the results. Fierce and cruel, she is part of this world and part of the underworld; she laughs heartily and heartlessly. This is one of the best paintings I have ever done, both technically and spiritually, and having completed it, I may never paint again.

That thought, fleeting as it is, does not bother me nearly as much as our aborted trips to Santa Fe. Something dark crushes me each time I think I may not be meant to go back there. Although we've rescheduled our departure for the end of the week, I fear we may be derailed once again. Finding omens in the shapes of clouds and stones, I expect any moment to hear a vindictive god saying, "You can't have a life in New Mexico. You've left that land, so you've no right to think you can just turn around and go back to it."

Fear is strangling me, fueled no doubt by a recent series of violent crimes in Tucson. The one that sent me over the edge was a carjacking in which a single mom my age was killed upon resisting a sexual assault. When I go out in public with my daughter, I scan our surroundings for danger of the worst sort. When we're in the car, I obsess over how to rescue her if someone should appear at my window with a gun. I am armed, as if living in a war zone.

Rape, murder, and numerous other atrocities are corroding the soul of this nation. Our citizens have gone mad with the taste of blood. Yet if the Berlin Wall can come down, miracles can happen here too.

December 20, 1992

The pileup of recent events has pushed me face-first into a quagmire of emotional goo. With Christmas rapidly approaching, I've begun canceling social obligations and refusing invitations. It feels better to do less, considering the decreased contact I now have with my inner world, which leaves me only half alive. Where have all my helpful spirits fled to?

Although I have temporarily retired from painting, I continue to work with oil pastels in my sketchbook. Last week I captured a beautiful image of two women standing out in the high desert of New Mexico. One, wrapped tightly in a blanket, is looking toward the mountains in front of her; the other, dressed in white, is gazing over her left shoulder at distant mesas. I want to be where they are, standing barefoot in the dust.

If only some wise woman would tell me not to waste my time worrying! I want to know that the house is going to sell at just the right moment and that we will be able to afford a home with a good roof, a splendid bathtub, a fireplace, and large, airy rooms to work in. I could pay a psychic to tell me these things or I could go horseback riding with my ears wide open. Tomorrow I will go to the stables in search of a smart horse.

December 23, 1992

It's nearly freezing outside, and at 12:30 A.M. I'm too stirred up to sleep. Christmas has me more excited than I've been in years. Why? Because the kid is old enough to appreciate it and my brother's here visiting. Ghosts are here, too, so there's been some crying mixed in with the excitement.

Last night I dreamed I was in the backyard of the house I grew up in. Peering through the darkness, I could barely make out the silhouettes of four or five coyotes trapped in the yard. As one of them followed me around a bend, Bob took off after it. "She'll be dangerous if you corner her!" I called out. Then Bella took off after Bob. "Don't let Bella fight with the coyote—one of them will get hurt," I added. But before I could say another word, Sasha raced around the bend after them.

Sure enough, Sasha was bitten. Although what she had was a pressure bite rather than a puncture wound, I was very upset and called the police. Two officers soon arrived, one of whom was extremely skeptical; no matter what I said, he didn't believe me. I tried to convince him of the terrible danger in our midst, explaining that in years past I'd seen coyotes running down Rodeo Drive carrying dead cats. "Do something or I'll be out here with a gun," I threatened. I didn't want it to come to that; I merely wanted the coyotes moved to a safer place.

Each time I puzzle over the meaning of this dream, I think of the coyotes' capacity for survival and adaptability. Since in the dream these ghostly animals that I usually view as allies turned on me, it seems to suggest that some of my survival instincts have turned on me. Perhaps I have become *too* adaptable. In trying to shut down the strong homing instinct pulling me to New Mexico, I may be ignoring an inner knowing of what's right for me.

A second aspect of my personality was depicted by the unsympathetic cop who doubted me, trying to talk me out of knowing what I knew and asking for what I needed. He was cold and mean, and he considered me a nuisance—much like I sometimes treat myself. On another level, I see that I am frightened by the coyote nature of life, terrified of being at the mercy of the sometimes cruel twists and turns of fate.

In short, this dream is warning me that I am in danger, that frightening things are happening in the darkness and no one is taking them seriously. My job is to stop doubting myself, stand by what I know to be true, and resist the fear that comes down on me so hard. Spiritually, it is a matter of life and death to believe that God is going to take me by the hand and lead me wherever I am supposed to go.

Chapter 13

A New Year Begins

Tucson, Arizona
January 1, 1993

Last night Bob and I stayed up until midnight writing down everything we wanted to leave behind in the months to come. We then burned our lists. Next we jotted down everything we wanted to materialize in the months ahead. Those lists we read to each other while drinking bottles of cold sparkling cider. It was a fine way to celebrate the new year.

Come morning, Janee and I painted. I began a new piece in the Soft Rocks series—a sequence I last worked on more than four years ago. It's fascinating how a series of paintings surfaces, runs along for a while, then returns to the underground river until years later when another image suddenly breaks through. I love the idea of soft rocks and keep several of these paintings hanging in the house because they are so soothing.

A four year old is currently on my lap drawing pictures of ant homes, ants wrapped in spiderwebs, baby ants, and ant "police" with big pincers. Not only is this a clumsy, inefficient, wonderful way to write but I have to stop every so often to play a round or two of bug dominoes—a game that has replaced the traditional dots of dominoes with grasshoppers, beetles, bees, and ants all painted on wooden blocks. At the present moment, my young assistant is crawling on the office floor with a magnifying glass, looking for lost pens, paper clips, and feathers while granting me the luxury of a completed paragraph.

January 5, 1993

I've just dreamed of having an art show in my living room studio. Although it was empty of furniture and paintings were hanging everywhere, only a few people showed up. Toward the end of the show, I noticed guests I had not seen before and realized they must have come at the last possible moment. "I'm sick of people invading my space," I said to myself. "I'll shut down as planned. I don't want them to own my paintings anyway."

While wandering around muttering to myself, I suddenly felt an evil presence in the house. Approaching me was an African man wearing a backpack and holding a doll my aunt Edgarita had brought me from Germany when I was a child. The doll had blonde, wavy, soft hair and a lovely expression on her face; I used to long to be as beautiful as her when I grew up. This man, however, had taken my old doll and refurbished her, painstakingly refashioning her body out of soft, shiny fabric and giving her a new dress. He handed her to me as if she were a treasure.

Although she was indeed beautiful and had been turned into a splendid renovation of her former self, I didn't feel good about his offering. As a number of people began gathering around us, oohing and ahhing over the exquisite doll, I asked myself, "Why don't I trust this man? Why am I always so damn suspicious?"

I then noticed several parrot feathers protruding from his backpack. Sensing that an object jammed inside the pack was wanting to jump out, I embarked on a spirit calling. Singing a snake song and imitating the *ch-ch-ch-ch-ch* of a rattler, I began a writhing limbolike dance around the man's legs. All the while a power inside me was willing whatever was vibrating beneath the feathers to magically wriggle up out of the backpack and into my hands.

The unseen forces I had summoned assisted me in snatching the vibrating object from the pack: it was the real German doll run through with long needles! Without hesitation, I plucked each one from her body. "You son of a bitch," I yelled at the man. "Get out of my house!" He fled into the night.

How can I continue to exhibit my work after a dream like this? The house reeks of the sage I have burned to purify my studio. I must make sure my old dolls are bolted down, or at least stowed safely away.

I have finished the small soft rock painting, and also another cross painting. That one surprised me, for I had assumed the cross series had run its course. But no—once I had a good layer of paint formed into an upright beam, it was immediately traversed by a horizontal one, whereupon small ears of yellow, red, and blue corn began piling themselves up in the center of it all and a border of pink zigzags appeared. This cross, like the others, evokes the same healing, centering effect as a meditation. I feel more grounded now.

February 14, 1993

The short days of winter are drawing to a close, and it is time to celebrate the return of light. In honor of the occasion, I went to the local church on February 1 to take part in an improvised celebration for women. Although we each had different views and desires, we devised a beautiful ceremony, burning red candles, chanting, and dancing.

Because it was bone-chilling cold, I had brought a black blanket with stripes of turquoise, red, pink, and yellow, which I kept wrapped around me the entire time. At first I covered everything but my eyes and took on the spirit of one of the desert women I had been drawing. As the music accelerated, I began flying around the room with the blanket flapping behind me. "Put the blanket down. No one else is dancing with a blanket," said my inner critic. "What do you think you look like?" But these puny human objections fell into the great abyss, for I was someone else and all I could do was dance wildly.

Having been transported to an otherworldly sphere, I was incapable of directing my movements—a powerlessness that often occurs when I dance. Usually, the hair all over my body stands on end and goose bumps cover my arms; soon afterward, I find I have grown coyote ears, bird wings, or fish scales. My job is simply to get out of the way.

This time, as the ritual continued, I saw myself, as if from a great distance, wrapped in a black blanket with stripes of many colors. The next day, while drawing three women standing in the desert at the foot of blue mesas, I noticed that one of them faced away from me, speaking quietly to the other two. She wore the black blanket.

February 22, 1993

I've been assaulted by a serious bout of asthma, and the medicine makes me sick. After two and a half hours of lying in wait for sleep, I have given up and come into my office to welcome the rising sun.

Yesterday Bob and I went to see the movie *Howard's End,* a compelling story about the power of place. On our way back to the hacienda, as dramatic shadows moved along the ridges of the Catalinas, I wept. If my doctor told me that *I* was about to die, I wondered, would I choose to live out my days in Tucson or Santa Fe? The answer was clear: I would pack up my family, gather together the dogs and cats and my paints, and begin the journey home. Immediately upon my arrival I would start a big painting of the three women in the desert.

February 24, 1993

I've had a beautiful day with Jean Marie! Despite my decision never to paint again, we went to paint pictures of the rocks in Texas Canyon—one of those spectacular gardens of stone unique to the West. The rocks were stacked in strange and wild combinations: dinosaur eggs, women packed together like sardines, even Henry Moore sculptures.

While searching for a place to perch, I came upon four cardinal feathers in the shade of an oak tree. For years I had been hunting for a scarlet feather, so imagine my delight at finding four of them—a splendid gift from the universe! Sensitive to messages relayed through special feathers, I heard the words, "You are walking the right path."

Jean Marie and I were absorbed in the rocks and pleased with the work that come out. After about two hours of painting and sketching, we felt the wind begin to rise and headed back to the van to picnic on French baguettes, Gouda, and Brie. Then we wandered through a desolate yet beautiful graveyard, reading names inscribed long ago and crying inexplicably over the dead. As we set off for home, the skies opened up, dropping torrents of rain on the earth. All in all, it was one of those great painting days that artists live for.

February 25, 1993

This morning before the sun rose, I walked the dogs to the road to get the newspaper, all the while saying morning prayers and handing my day over to God. Suddenly, I heard a piercing, rasping animal sound from somewhere close by. Turning slowly in a circle, I caught the form of a large Harris' hawk on one of the nearby telephone poles. From a clump of trees came the sweeping movement of a second hawk elegantly sailing toward the one perched on the pole. With the precision that typifies a bird of prey, he lowered himself onto his female partner, whereupon their great wings fanned out around their tipping bodies. Gazing at their magnificent silhouette against the pale morning sky, I witnessed an act that may well lead to the creation of a family of hawks.

Later in the morning I looked out the bedroom window to find the pair—or perhaps a second couple—intertwined on another telephone pole. Dense screening from the eucalyptus tree enabled Bob and Sasha to see this extraordinary mating event without disturbing the winged lovers.

March 3, 1993

I have been so busy working and avoiding work that I've not been keeping up with my writing. A fascinating series of events began a few days ago when I placed an ad at the University of Arizona job center: "Wanted—genealogist. Looking for my family." Right away, I received a call from someone interested in the search. "I was so surprised to see your ad," the man said. "Genealogy searches are what I do! I'm an anthropologist."

Yesterday he visited, and we began a quest for the lost Sioux grandmother who had hair, eyes, and cheekbones like mine. I dug out marriage licenses, birth certificates, and notes from my brother, who years ago began recording fragments of family history. Although I do not expect to find this woman, I am looking just the same.

When the genealogist left, I called my brother, and together we made a little map of all the family members we could think of, where they were born, and which of the males had more than one wife at a time. We started with Dorothy June Thompson, my mother, and Ferris Maynard Webster, my father. We knew their parents: on my mother's side, David Archer Thompson (born in Salt Lake City, Utah) and Nina June Chrome (born in Fairfield, Illinois), one of the patron saints of codependency; on my father's side, Edgar Lincoln Webster (birthplace unknown) and Annie Ranahan (born in Canada), a woman considerably his junior, whom he married promptly after her emergence from convent school. He had wooed her mother for a number of years during Annie's absence. Annie's mother's maiden name was Brigette O'Brannigan (born in County Cork, Ireland).

Edgar Lincoln Webster's mother is the woman we are hunting for. We do not know her name, but she is said to be Sioux—a Santee. According to my brother's research, she was most likely a member of the Midewakanton (Spirit or Lake Dwellers), Wahpeton (Leaf Dwellers), Sisseton (Fish-Scale Dwellers), or Wahpekute (Leaf Shooters) clan. A family story was often told of a day when Edgar Lincoln was in his cradle and his father was off hunting. While Edgar and his mother were alone in the cabin, several Indians came to the door. She fed them and gave them coffee; they ate, drank, and left in peace.

My mother's kin have been more accessible to me. Her mother's family extends back to John Chrome, an American painter of some renown. I once saw his moody, dark landscapes in California's Huntington Museum, and immediately resonated with the spirit in the work, particularly his love of trees. Then there's my great-aunt Pearl, my grandmother's sister, long considered extremely unattractive and unmarriagable, yet bighearted. To everyone's surprise, she enjoyed a brief romance and eventually marriage with a man named Claude Stogsdill, who soon afterward was gassed in World War I. Her joy ended in years of dreary caregiving for Claude, and ultimately in his death. Oh, but Pearl could sew! A true artist, she sewed from her lonely heart.

For as long as I can remember, my mother had an unfinished quilt Pearl had made. After my mother's death, Janee introduced me to a woman who finished that quilt, bringing a forgotten work of beauty to completion and at the same time preserving fragments of a family that had been dropping dead like flies.

March 15, 1993

When I was in my early thirties, I had a Big Dream. A dark force was searching for me outside my childhood home, which my paternal grandparents had built and died in. I was running frantically through the house trying to extinguish each light so that the cunning dark being would not be able to locate me. At last, a disembodied voice explained, "You will always be hunted down because of the power that was passed down to you through the ancient bloodlines of your Celtic grandmother, her mother, and her mother before her." I felt the blood of all these women banging in my veins.

I feel their blood now as vigorously as I did then. Through them I hear someone calling me, and I am listening. Great-Grandmother, I am coming after you. I do not expect to find you, but I know I am supposed to try.

March 16, 1993

I have returned from another magnificent trip to Texas Canyon—for a "paint out" with several of my women students. They quickly became lost in this painter's wonderland, and I fell down the rabbit hole after them. I had a hell of a time tracking them down after they went into the bushes to find their spots to paint. Artists are like that.

The rocks in our little cove were superanimated. The oak trees stood quietly guarding them, catching the wind. It is a fascinating place for painting if rocks are your passion.

March 18, 1993

Looking out the kitchen window to the telephone pole, I see another Harris' hawk surveying the landscape from what has become a favorite roost. The female often waits there for the male, who then swoops down upon her. Immediately, they proceed to enact their own rites of spring, determined to replenish the earth with their aristocratic offspring.

The morning air is silver-pink and cool enough to warrant an oversized Irish sweater. The prickly pear cactus are covered with small green nubs waiting to explode into luscious flowers. Beneath them, the earth is vibrant. Spring stalks flamboyantly across the desert.

Looking through the storage closet for my father's death certificate, which I promised to give the genealogist, I moved aside a mirror that sits on a cherry-wood dresser my mother gave me when I was a child. There behind the mirror was a family Bible belonging to my father's mother, Annie Ranahan—an item I had not seen in at least twenty years. Inside were notations on the birth of my grandparents whose eventual marriage marked the union of the Sioux and Celtic bloodlines that run through me. Although I have no idea how this relic found its way to Tucson, I feel several footsteps closer to Great-Grandmother. She is leading me to her.

Sensing her presence at this moment, I ask aloud, "Why have I not been contacted by my mother?" Her reply: "She belongs to your father—always did. *You* belong to *us*." I know in the ancient chambers of my being that this is so, for my connection with these women fills a portion of the void left by my parents' departure. While searching for them, I feel less like an orphan.

March 20, 1993

The wheel of the year has come full circle today, as have many of the threads weaving in and out of my life. At 6:00 A.M. I picked up Patria, a wise woman from Taos whom I've recently met, and headed out into the Catalinas. There we drummed together until the sun rose burning and golden over the eastern ridge of the Rincons. The mosquitoes were monstrously large and overly friendly—so much so that every now and then we ended up smashing them with our beaters. *Bang, bang, bang, smash. Bang, bang, bang, smash.* A four-beat time signature is ideal for drumming in the equinox, whether or not you are plagued with mosquitoes.

While drumming, I stared at the little old moon grazed by veils of pink clouds, as it hung in the lightening sky. I watched until it was not there anymore.

Once the sun was up, we left for Patria's guesthouse, where she showed me photographs of her mesa-top home in Taos, New Mexico. I marveled that both of us have been "assigned" to Tucson and are waiting for the next shuttle bound for the red earth of New Mexico. While waiting, I thought, let's have a little cry, a ritual cleansing, shall we? And so we did—we sat on the bed and let it rip. Bringing in the equinox with a radiant woman in her seventh decade of life let me know that we are on the trail together even though she is several paces ahead of me.

Upon returning home, I advanced to the next stage of letting go of my very dead parents by placing a call to the woman who brings the Casas Grandes pots up from Mexico. Arriving at her home, I picked out the perfect container for my parents' ashes; it was just the right size and was painted red and black on an earthen field. Putting their ashes in the pot is the next step in this ritual. Before the first new moon of spring, there will indeed be a change of residence for what's left of Mom and Dad.

I can feel a deluge of work coming through the birth canal. A dark man has been pursuing me in my dreams. Along with his spiderwebs and feathers, what gifts and stories will he bring?

March 21, 1993

This evening the family went out into the desert with the red-and-black pot, rattles, incense, and two heavy boxes of ashes. When we came to a small clearing among the cactus, I lit some cedar. The smoke swirled around us and upward, letting me know it was praying time. We then took a handful of ashes from each box and cast them into the cedar-laden wind that whipped around us. Alternately, I poured into the pot some of my father's ashes and some of my mother's, as if following an old family recipe. While I poured, Sasha and Bob rattled and called the spirits. At that point, the wind roared and lightning crashed around us. *Chh-chh-chh* went the rattles, accompanying the thunder. When the boxes were empty, I joined in the rattling and the calling.

For about twenty minutes, the dust rose out of the mouth of the pot like a small tornado. "Good-bye, my dearest friends who gave me the gift of life, art, passion, and stylish eccentricity," I intoned. "Lovers for over fifty years, you are together again."

When the work was done, the rains fell. On our way home, I envisioned carrying the pot out into the mountains above Santa Fe some day and setting those ashes free.

Chapter 14

The Three Wise Women

Tucson, Arizona
March 24, 1993

I've spent the afternoon frenetically preparing paintings for an informal exhibit at the same downtown furniture showroom as before. After painting the edges of the canvases, and fastening eyes and wires to the back of each one, I compiled my price list, crammed all the paintings I could into the car, and delivered the work—completing in several hours an ordeal that normally takes two weeks.

Although I don't expect to sell anything at this exhibit, I periodically like to clear the studio walls for a while. Then I paint happily into the void.

March 25, 1993

It's 5:00 A.M. and I've just padded down the hall in the dark, slamming into a wall. As soon as the "shooting stars" stopped, I made my way to the kitchen for some ice.

On the easel in the studio was "The Three Women," completed and altogether haunting. The earth beneath the figures was a strange composite of writhing lines and colors. The figures themselves are women I have seen in my mind for years. Eternally engaged in conversation, they watch and tell their stories. Sometimes guides and at other times harpies, they are demanding teachers. If I take time to listen to them, they have all the information I need. But if I do not heed their words, nothing can rescue me from their talons.

Soon this painting will go up on one of the newly blank walls of the house, and another will take its place on the easel. In fact, propped against the adobe walls outside the front door are several dozen blank canvases. I haven't put them in the barn because I like to see them waiting each time I open the door. I like to know I am rich in canvas!

One of them will become a painting for the editor of a Virginia Beach newspaper who has commissioned a piece with a lion and the sun. I don't usually take commissioned work unless clients specify only the size of the piece and otherwise give me free rein, but in this instance the symbols were pleasing to me and began sparking ideas. Tomorrow I'll go to the library for reference photos, then I'll incubate the images. Eventually, the little machine that's inside the artist will go *click-click-click* and spit out the picture.

April 15, 1993

A viral assault is ravaging the family, keeping me at home to provide solace and nurturing. But I'd like to be out in the desert, which at this moment is softly painted in silver. I'd like to take my drum, as well as Patria and her drum, and go *bang-bang-bang-bang* in a cave, diving deep into the earth to the breast of the Great Mother. There I would saturate my being with color and merge with the erratic feminine spirit.

Almost every day I paint those women I have seen thousands of times—my wise women, my seers. I paint them over and over, trying to capture their every turn, the angle of their heads in conversation, the stance of their bodies. These women insist on being painted in the landscape where they are rooted as if growing from the red-and-purple earth amid mesas, twisted canyons, and convoluted arroyos filled with old bones.

"Well, *comadres,* I am watching, paintbrush in hand," I say to them silently. *"¡Vámanos!"* Then as I open myself to the river of images, I see women everywhere in the desert—women with horses, women watching impassively, women in the clouds and rocks, women who are mountains, and women who are storms. Surrendering to creativity is an awesome and fearful process.

May 8, 1993

We're back from two weeks of travel—first to London to put on a workshop, then to Italy to see my niece Kris. Buzzing with jet lag and the aftereffects of travel with an energetic five year old, I started cleaning the house at 6:00 A.M. Knee-deep in laundry and Arizona grime, I vacuumed, dusted, ripped out old plants and put in new ones, then ran eight loads of laundry after gathering clothes that had been draped over every available chair, door, and cabinet knob. Once the sun was up, I marketed, banked, and sorted through the stacks of mail that had accumulated.

At 1:00 P.M. I drove to school to scoop up the kid and another wild child. When they quieted down to play cards, I slipped away to write—until silence got the best of my curiosity. Following a newly laid path of gray footprints, I found the girls in the bathroom, where they had "painted" the sink and some houseplants with white glue. The kitchen, den, and bathroom reminded me of a scene from the fifties, with footprints leading across the floor, up a wall, across the ceiling, and back down the facing wall.

While driving Sasha's buddy home, I suddenly wondered what they had put their feet into and if it would ever come off. Something must have distracted me, however, for I never popped the question. I suspect I have grown as a mother because I did not worry that whatever it was might eat their feet off.

Upon our return home, I spent several more hours fixing the mess, and by the time Bob came in I was frothing. "Hi, honey! How was your day?" he asked, chipper as could be. He was offended when flames shot out of my mouth.

It's hard to get back to center after a two-week break. Yet ironically, the distractions that interrupted my earlier attempt to write have since become a crooked little doorway back to that quiet place where I can listen to myself. I needed to write about my frustrations; I must always start with where I am in the present moment.

The trip not only threw me off center but also interrupted the flow of imagery that had been bubbling up within me. While working in oil pastels earlier this evening, I could see the wrapped women walking toward dark mesas, but I could not see their faces. Nor have they told me what they know. I must patiently keep working in my sketchbook, sweeping the floor, tending the garden—all the while waiting for them to turn and face me. Observing them in constant conversation, I feel left out.

May 9, 1993

It's Mother's Day and this mother has been up with her child since 5:30 in the morning. Sasha's now off in the kitchen gathering materials for a homemade bird feeder—paper, tape, and no doubt a lot more birdseed than I want to know about. I have willingly traded a few minutes to myself for the chaotic results of unsupervised play. When you let a child express herself, your world gets messy.

The director of a respected local gallery phoned yesterday, wanting to show some of my work. You could have knocked me over with a hard breath! It's been years since I've had so much as a nibble from a gallery.

May 18, 1993

I'm sitting under a mesquite tree in sizzling heat, waiting for Heidi to come. Nearby, beautiful pale pink oleander trees are nodding in the breeze now filled with songs from dozens of birds. They are happy just to be alive, and so am I. I am coming unstuck. I can feel the barnacles falling off as I prepare to slide through the water. I'm getting ready to move on to the next era, the next me.

Inspired by my niece's neat and orderly house in Italy, I have tended to my own, dusting and vacuuming everything that doesn't have a tail. Winter quilts have been pulled from the beds for airing or cleaning. Broken objects have been fixed, painted, prettied, or pulverized. How I'm enjoying the fruits of these labors!

While studying the painting of the three desert women as it simmers on the easel, I've noticed that their path is circular. Regardless of the direction they choose to go in, they will end up where they are. They can even separate and go in different directions and *still* reach their destination. In effect, they cannot choose the wrong path.

What about me—am I going to lose *my* way? Not right now. Even in my profoundly unknowing state, I can feel the hand of God steering my life. No longer am I fretting, questioning, or fighting. I've stopped playing with "where," and "when" is not bothering me at the moment. I'm staying in the present tense and letting my life unfold, aware that something bigger than me is pushing the water downriver.

I am living each day as if I will be in Tucson forever. Should I be guided elsewhere, I will recognize the primordial call and answer it.

May 22, 1993

It's Saturday night, Bob's been out of town for days, and I'm home with Sasha. She's sleeping so soundly that a brass band would not disturb her. Around midnight, she'll most likely sleepwalk down the hall and climb into my bed—a nightly pilgrimage that's been going on since she figured out how to climb out of her crib.

My plan for the evening entailed chasing giant dog-hair balls around the house with a miracle appliance I bought today—an electric broom that resembles a cross between a vacuum cleaner and a vibrator. It had so much horsepower that I envisioned putting a saddle blanket on it and riding it around the house . . . *Eeehah!* Eventually identifying my evening ambitions as a warning sign of creeping dementia, I unplugged the broom and headed for the writing table. The furry balls will just have to blow around like tumbleweeds a little longer.

In addition to purchasing a modern convenience, I spent the day creating an index for the next printing of *Warrior Woman.* The assignment came from Alex, the guardian angel who has overseen the production of my book, guiding me every step of the way. "An index helps sell a book," he explained. He tries hard to keep things simple for me, and has managed to interpret every little note about my life that I've crammed into grubby, sweat-drenched envelopes and mailed to him from one address after another while hopscotching my way across the great Southwest painting, writing, and looking for myself. If he could do that, I figured, surely I could compile an index.

May 24, 1993

It's 9:00 A.M. and hot as hell. Mourning doves are *hoo-hoo*ing in the mesquite. A century plant is erecting a flower at great altitude outside my office window. And I am relishing the wonderful time I had yesterday with the house to myself.

I spent the day doing my favorite thing: goofing off. Because there were no people waiting for breakfast, and no piles of dirty dishes or underwear to deal with, showering became a sensuous luxury. After showering, I wandered aimlessly through stores, carting around stacks of books, bolts of fabrics, and racks of skirts, all the while engaging in odd conversations with people I didn't know, even making them laugh. I love touching fabrics of all kinds and picking up little trinkets, turning them over in my hand, then setting them back down. Returning home, I took a naked dip in the pool under the late afternoon sky, a divine immersion. By evening, I was ready to write.

What is so satisfying about writing? Why do I come to it with such enthusiasm and need? Writing convinces me that I am making a difference in the world. With either pen in hand or keyboard purring, I come to my creative life like a child entering a secret playroom: the farther in she steps, the more absorbed she becomes in the delicious treasures that abound there. So it is that soon after I sit down to write, I am often out of my own way and words are flowing through me. Oh, I live for such days of contentment!

May 26, 1993

This morning I need to write so I can see what's swirling under the surface and then empty the bucket. With most of my creativity going into indexing, linear shapes and ideas are buzzing around under my beret. It's hard to get anything else done . . . It's certainly hard to have fun.

May 29, 1993

I've added a few desert plants to the latest rendition of the three women. Seeing these little plants reminds me of the time I found my paintings littered with bones. At first, I was apprehensive. "Just paint the damn things," I told myself. "Don't waste energy asking why. The asking is only a delay, like a kid wanting a glass of water, a tissue, and a back rub to avoid going to bed. Just paint the images. Maybe you'll figure out their meaning later; maybe not." Later, when people in my life started dying, the images made sense.

So it is with these plants and the women who walk beside them. In one painting after another I see them turning this way and that, conversing quietly among themselves, and sometimes arguing as they walk along the path. Every time I set my hands to paper, they come. The moment I close my eyes, there they are, working things out for me. Their collective feminine wisdom is doing for me what I cannot do for myself in the linear world. They are the *curanderas*, the inner guides who await me at all the crossroads of my journey.

The desert breeze has set the wind chimes to singing outside my window. Although temperatures are hovering around 100 degrees, I keep the windows open and rely on the swamp cooler to create tolerable indoor temperatures. With the windows ajar, the penetrating electric buzz of cicadas and the trilling of desert birds fill the house with riotous sounds of nature.

Her sights are equally glorious. Not ten feet from me is a brilliant red-orange cactus flower, and high in the tall cholla next to it is the nest of a cactus wren. The shimmying fernlike shade of the mesquite trees breaks the harshness of the midday sun, lending a lacy quality to the moving patterns of light and shadow.

Will I leave this house or will I stay? The answer to that riddle is part of what's been turned over to the desert women. I love it here, especially in this room where my mother spent her last days; but it is equally important to recognize that my heart and roots are in Santa Fe.

Until a moment ago I was waiting for a call about a visitor to the studio. The call has just come through—a cancellation!—and my day has opened up before me. There is no place I have to go, no one to see, no errands to run, no dinner to cook . . . a gift from the universe.

For months I've been working hard to achieve freedom from houseguests, phone calls, meaningless social obligations, and errands. At the same time, a cattle prod deep within me has kept me running from morning till night. Recognizing how pressured and angry I have been feeling, I've decided to diligently enforce a campaign of "disexcellence."

This need for more freedom was signaled not only by my explosive temper but by my observations of numerous brilliant, gifted, overachieving women who refuse to cut themselves any slack. Most of my women friends are either in school full-time or holding jobs and parenting kids—both of which leave them too exhausted to attend to their own needs and interests. All this emphasis on achievement is taking the fun out of their lives. Surely, some people were designed to run on the fast track, but it's killing the rest of us. As for me, I'm determined to labor intensively at being more of a slob!

June 3, 1993

It has been a day full of emotion. When I dropped Sasha off at preschool this morning, I realized that her time there was drawing to a close. On my way back to the car, I began weeping out of gratitude for her teacher, Pam. It is hard to leave someone who has been a good teacher to your child.

Painting class started late today. Laurie, a steady student and joy in my life, was settled in and working contemplatively when Frances came in and curled up on the couch for a good cry. About ten minutes later Lis, a dancer who has been painting with me for several months, came through the door, saying, "I just wanted to let you know I can't get it together to paint today." Unruffled, I asked, "Where's Julia Rose?" Her stellar new baby, it turned out, was in the car. "Bring her in and sit on the couch with us for a minute," I suggested. With Julia indoors, safely ensconced in her car seat, Lis burst out crying and rolled up in a ball. Some classes do need to be structured differently from others, I thought to myself.

After a good long time, we mopped up. "Before you go," I

announced, "let's use paper and oil pastels to make one image that will be like a journal entry portraying how you are feeling right now."

As soon as they set to work, images and colors poured out of them, which is what often happens just when you think your students are about to throw the net over you. What counts in class is not how many hours you spend painting, but rather how much courage you have to grab your raw creative energy by the tail.

June 5, 1993

Last night I went out to soak under the full moon. While floating in the hot water, I recited made-up poems about the moon's beauty. The words came out hesitant and overblown, and the verses were sticky. Still, it felt good to recite atrocious poetry.

Before climbing into bed, I made sure the shutters were open so moonbeams could wash over us in our sleep. Then at 5:00 A.M. I stepped outside to watch the lunar eclipse. Naked, I wrapped my arms around myself and searched for the moon, but it had set below the horizon. Although I'd missed the main attraction of the night, I felt energized by what I could not see.

Each time I pick up my pad and start drawing in oil pastels, the three women appear. They are so busy working things out in the caverns of my psyche that nothing else comes through. These women are big, soft rocks that have been sitting in the desert for centuries, and now they have stood up and started walking toward the mesas.

Deep beneath the surface, I am changing. I still take great pleasure in turquoise, lavender, and the song of mourning doves; and I continue to be influenced by phases of the moon. But at times I don't want to paint, and for days on end I don't write. Instead, I am remembering how to *live*.

June 9, 1993

I am in extreme discomfort. No food tastes good; there's nothing I want; I am lost and stuck; and I don't like myself. Why? Who knows—I've been spending too much time trying to figure out what's wrong.

One thing I do know is that Bob has forgotten his deep love for New Mexico. Lately, he's been muttering that Santa Fe is turning cosmopolitan and that he does not want to live in *la villa commerciale.* This state of affairs depresses me, since for nearly five years I have clung to the hope of returning to live there as if it were the Promised Land. I'm suffering from "dying dream syndrome."

To escape the inferno of Tucson, we are planning to spend a week in New Mexico next month. Perhaps that visit will resolve the ongoing quandary about the next step in our lives. But what will happen if my inner guidance tells me it's time to go home and Bob disagrees? Or if I find that I've outgrown my dream? After all, it's hard to hold to a vision over such an extended absence, especially when you're no longer the person who incubated it. Either discovery would leave me flattened out, defeated. Exacerbating my dying dream syndrome is an acute bout of "exile's warping of the heart."

In this unhappy state I have started a six-week creativity support group. Five people have signed up to talk about ideas, express fears, and share works in progress.

Also on the horizon is a talk I'm scheduled to give in California. My real purpose in going is to see Jeanne; as for speaking, I'm not the least bit interested. I seem to be at an emotional impasse. Everyday life looks bleak.

June 14, 1993

I miss living near Jeanne, especially when the "earth starts shifting." As soon as she wrapped her arms around me, I knew the speaking engagement would go well. And it did, thanks to the transfusion from my dear friend.

The first meeting of the creativity support group was a success, too. We talked about avoidance techniques—how artists and other creative people find a million things to do in the course of a day to refrain from plunging into their creativity. Artistic creatives, we discovered, are adept at finding culprits to blame for our lack of immersion and then sitting back and pretending to be trapped in defeat. In effect, we dig a dark little pit, jump in, and wallow in the belief that we *can't* create because of our husband, wife, children, job, or lack of money for supplies. The truth is that we have the ability to turn *anything* into an avoidance technique.

A more liberating truth is that beneath creative inaction lies a layer of anger, and beneath the anger, a power plant of creativity. Blasting away some of the anger emancipates the creativity. Ignoring the phone and turning off the TV frees up more than enough time for letting off the steam.

After last week's group, I wrote like a mad thing. I scribbled on scraps of paper. While running errands with Heidi, I filled blank pages in the back of her real estate listings. I wrote before giving my talk; then I threw my notes away, knowing the words would come out fine.

I also made a drawing of one of the desert women. She was walking along a chartreuse road, her face barely formed, with only a hint of features. She is somewhere between who she was and who she will be next.

All my visual work currently consists of oil pastel drawings on paper. The colors are brilliant and, with manipulation, can be neutralized or muted, lending themselves to a vital means of expression. I keep a pad ready; I dump pastels on the table; I begin to draw. As long as images come out, I know I'm going to end up in the right place.

June 16, 1993

This week's group meeting was rich. We discussed what it is like to write every day. Daily writing, we found, greases the creative channels and has tremendous medicinal value as well, especially in alleviating emotional blockage and creative constipation.

The work we do together is stream-of-consciousness writing, with no correcting and no rules. Whatever needs to come out comes out. If participants say they can't write, we write about not writing—the scary part, the bad part, the plumbing, then on to the guts, the soul, the secrets. "Grab the demons by the throat and search for God," I tell them. "Rant, rave, froth, be sappy, look stupid."

Between meetings, group members are encouraged to attend art shows, readings, book signings, and concerts. Supporting presenting artists integrates us into the art community. Participating in the worlds of music, dance, visual arts, and poetry feeds us as artists.

Breaking the habit of non-self-nurturance requires that all the old wiring be ripped out and new tapes made to replace the old. New tapes hinge on a commitment to take action. People who want to create have to drag their tired asses to that African dance class they want to investigate, then get up and join the dancers. Because the nurturing of creativity has practically been bred out of us, it takes great courage to step forth in this way when you think you should really be home doing the laundry.

I practice this discipline myself. I find out something of interest that's going on in the art community, then I get in my car and go. Most often I travel solo so I can absorb the experience free of distraction and chatter, and I stay until I'm finished; rarely do I speak about these adventures. This week, for example, I took a few minutes to visit a painting I like—to absorb its strength and color. Photography shows yield good results, too.

We close each group meeting by going around the circle and making a commitment to our art for the week. When we commit to an easily accomplished goal, the cumulative effect can be transformative. Simple actions bring profound change.

Part of my commitment this week was to call Dorothy Cannon, my painting teacher for more than fourteen years. How satisfying it was to hear her familiar voice after a twenty-year interlude! I asked if she was still teaching. "Yes," she said, "but I don't do as much for the kids anymore. I have them do more for themselves—which, as it turns out, is better for them."

That night I dreamed of a student asking Dorothy to look at a painting in progress. Gracefully, she turned and said, "Well, you could put a little more blue here. That would make the object appear to recede." Renewing contact with my former painting teacher reminded me of the enormous role she had played in helping me, and who knows how many others, to face life. She not only taught me how to paint but showed me how to live the life of an artist.

Norfolk, Virginia
June 27, 1993

I am here to give a talk tonight and a workshop tomorrow. The theme is "relationships"—a subject I am leery of addressing. What can I offer? I can say that I am Bob's seventh wife, that he doesn't pick up his socks, and that he doesn't clean up the dog poop in the yard unless I use a cattle prod. But how mundane that would be!

I have far more interesting things to say about our lives as two writers living together—about how I keep doing my art even with a family, and how we work down the hall from each other, calling out, "Is *assholes* two words, one word, or hyphenated?" and other questions, the asking and answering of which form a dance of love between us. I could say that I sometimes wake my husband up frantically at 2:00 A.M. to help me retrieve a paragraph I've lost in the computer, and that he doesn't get mad; to the contrary, he gets up good-naturedly and helps me. I could also say that evolving artistically is one of my primary jobs as a mother, and that making art is one of my daughter's favorite ways to play together. Art activity at home is giving her tools she will need to counteract the damage that will surely be visited on her creative spirit as she matures.

Most likely, I will talk about how I get myself up and moving, how I get the feelings flowing—by writing, stomping, bopping, singing, and writing every moment I can. I'll try to highlight four main points: that as I express myself, all my different selves and a variety of important information float up to the surface of my consciousness; that in clearing the clouds of discontent, I find out what I am feeling; that when I know what I am feeling in the hidden chambers of my heart, I know exactly what I need to do; and that without my art, I am one of the living dead.

Here in Norfolk, I am a morass of confused feelings. Tucson has loosened its hold on me, and I see that my untamed dogs need to run freely in thick winter coats while they are still young and full of life. Oregon is calling loud and clear; my last living aunt and my brother Peter live there, and it is where I spent every year of my childhood hunting with my dad. Yet Santa Fe still pulls at my heart, informing me that one day my home will once again be in the Sangre de Cristos, redolent with piñon smoke in the golden autumn.

To find relief from this horrible restlessness, I must assure myself that I will know where I am to spend the next portion of my life when I set foot there, as I did when I was led to my desert refuge in Tucson. My heart will surely tell me when I am home. Till then, I long for release from the craving to be apprised of my future. I know better than to move ahead of the hand of God.

Chapter 15

The Effects of Painting Power Masks

Tucson, Arizona
June 30, 1993

I am desperately adhering to traditional desert wisdom: up early in the morning, running errands in the evening, eating mostly fruit and vegetables. Even so, there's been no deliverance from this infernal heat!

Using oil pastels, I've been working on more find-myself portraits in the sketch pad. These unsettling pieces are mysterious, numinous, clear, and beginning to merge with the power-mask images. What once felt like a way to idly pass the time has taken on a life of its own. In fact, this series has evolved into what will probably be my next major tide in oil paintings. For artists, playing around is an investment.

While brushing paint thinner on one of these images earlier today, I recalled with a laugh how I accidentally began working in oil pastels. I needed a highly transportable medium to use with the workshop participants in Mexico. The oil pastels seemed like a good candidate—one easy enough for inexperienced artists to work with, as well as colorful enough to engage their attention. At first, I found them mildly interesting. But after several workshops went by, I realized I had stumbled upon a medium so malleable and fluid that I could get it to do almost anything; what's more, the sensual colors and textures were well suited to the strange, elusive imagery of the unconscious. Eventually I discovered that the images I drew from flickering visions and feelings translated easily into oil paint. After months of seemingly aimless play, I became intensely interested in my work again.

I now use the oil pastels to introduce new students to expressive art. All the vivid colors of the inner landscape are there in the little cardboard box.

This morning I had an urge to buy canvases, so I called a local art store to see if they had twenty-four-by-thirty-inch wrap-arounds. Yes, I was told, whereupon I hurried off into the heat, violating traditional desert precepts, only to find that they were out of twenty-four-by-thirty-inch canvases! Rather than return home empty-handed, I bought a big box of oil pastels containing a special turquoise the other sets don't have. These will keep me intrigued until I am able to track down some canvases.

July 6, 1993

To get myself to write, I've taken to bribery. Writing a full page entitles me to a lime Popsicle—a highly recommended option for those who don't drink Scotch. It's not lack of material that renders me indifferent to writing, but rather the physical effects of living in an inferno. The summer heat that leaves us all housebound except for a few precious predawn and postsunset hours is hell on a woman whose spiritual life is fed by hiking. I am in agony as the days stretch out longer and longer.

Painting, I trust, will not require an act of bribery. I ordered ten canvases from California that should be here any day now, and my plan is to paint some of the power masks I have sketched. Astonishing work comes from the practice of making one image a day.

July 13, 1993

During a recent sojourn in San Diego to put on an oversold women's workshop, I had a preworkshop interview with a local TV news broadcaster. Since she had asked me to bring artwork, and since I was reluctant to haul one of my six-foot jobs onto the plane, I took my drawing pads. I felt like a pip-squeak amid the slick TV people, yet the interviewer, although formidably polished, was gracious and thoughtful. So frightened was I by this gig that I had no qualms about the women's gathering.

Yesterday gave rise to another successful experience in the arts. The gallery lady who phoned me two months ago came for a two-hour visit. We poked through everything, even the barn, pulling pieces out under the mesquite trees. After years of trying, I am to be represented by a gallery!

Curiously, while lugging canvases out of the barn, I spotted a cactus wren feather on the ground—a postcard from the Great Spirit. I tucked the feather into the front of my concho belt, not realizing until much later that the cactus wren is the cosmic clown, the Fool.

July 17, 1993

Introducing the Pacific Northwest into the where-to-go enigma has added an element of excitement and mystery. Why consider such a place? In addition to the proximity of two of my three remaining family members, we've been mulling over the reasonable cost of homes there, the affordable land, the fact that our daughter will be starting kindergarten in the fall. We may well find ourselves on a path altogether different from the one I've been anticipating these five years in exile.

Now when I think of New Mexico, I fall to weeping. To me, she is the Great Mother, and I want nothing more than to rush into her arms and wet her dusty breast with my tears.

As it turns out, we will be traveling there once a month through October, because the universe has scheduled a series of combined social and business trips for us. Over these next few months, I hope to gather enough sustaining power to help me hold on to my dreams. Surely, one day this Tucson house will sell, whereupon I will pack my gilded Gypsy wagon and roll along dirt roads to my next destination.

My wandering spirit cannot rest once it knows the time has come to move on. When I get to where I'm going, this period of delay and frustration will no doubt make sense. Meanwhile, all I can do is pray for patience so the wild horse won't break her legs trying to jump the gate before it's been opened. "Wait, wild one," I tell myself. "Your time is coming. For now, keep your eye on the desert clouds."

Santa Fe, New Mexico
July 22, 1993

Dear God, I am in New Mexico, hoping that the Land of Enchantment will rekindle my husband's once passionate love of the place! These are my first moments alone since we rolled out of Tucson on an epic family production, complete with Barbie dolls and other props.

Later this morning Bob will be flying to Montana to speak, and taking Sasha with him. As the family files out, I am apt to tune into my inner voice, which has grown mute before the clamoring of my tribe. In their presence what I hear is, "I want milkie!" "Mommy, I spilled the cranberry juice!" "Where are my sunglasses, my keys, my shoes?"

I have been closely monitoring Bob's reaction to New Mexico and am scared that he has surely turned against the place because of all the trendy changes it has undergone since our departure. I've been taking his emotional pulse, searching his face, listening between his sentences, undertaking every sick thing you can do in a relationship. This external focus cuts me off from what I need to navigate most—namely, my own feelings.

Soon after Bob and Sasha left, I drove north to the old Santuario de Chimayó to pray for the relocation of my soul. On the way, I saw a white cross on a small hill. What actually caught my eye, and my imagination, were a series of impressions: red earth, a pale wash of sage green creeping up the hillside, a few piñon trees, and an enigmatic white cross with a long white scarf threaded through its circlet and whipping sensuously in the wind. The weathered cross seemed to have always been there, and I wondered who so carefully tended the white scarf that was flipping, flapping, snapping, and popping against the threatening gray skies.

New Mexico is indeed a place of mystery, thick with all manner of spirituality—some of it sacred, some profane. "It feels like home," my daughter said to me before leaving this morning. "I want to live here." I cannot help but agree, for I am stronger here, more whole, with bare feet planted in the dirt, face turned toward the high-desert wind.

July 24, 1993

The family has returned and is about to escort me to an appointment I've scheduled at a gallery to follow up on a referral. I am in an altered state—showered and perfumed, carrying my cellular phone (because I'm so very important) and my appointment book in a large, heavy bag. *Warrior Woman*'s in there, too. She often goes down the road ahead of me.

Tomorrow we leave for Tucson. I hope God will book a return engagement for me here, because this is where I want to do my painting. Although the place has changed during our five-year absence, so has the world . . . and so have I.

Tucson, Arizona
July 30, 1993

I am loaded with emotion. Just before leaving Santa Fe, Bob and I went with Jim Ratchford down an old Jeep road to look at some land in the foothills of the Sangre de Cristos. It was love at first sight. Something clicked inside me. Looking at Bob, I saw he was enraptured, so I pulled out the checkbook and bought the ground under our feet—two and a half acres about twenty minutes from the Plaza. Since we won't be able to build on the land until the Tucson house sells, we are planning to await the sale in a small Santa Fe adobe.

When the deal was signed, tears sprang forth, marking the end of a long and terrible struggle. I realized then how much energy had been bleeding out of me during these months of uncertainty. Taking action has renewed my strength. I did what I had to do to get myself and my family where we belong.

This afternoon Laurie came to paint. While we discussed my upcoming departure, she asked, "What's there that isn't here?" I told her, "It's inside stuff, not outside stuff. As for outside attractions, there's the red earth, the horizontal growth of the bushes, the sophisticated and rustic feel of the place. I fit there."

All my reservations have dissolved. I am more than ready to return to the place where cottonwood seeds sift to the earth like snow, thunder and lightning rack the land, and wind whips furiously around adobe houses—the place where my heart is steadfastly rooted.

July 31, 1993

Out my magical office window I am watching the last barrel cactus that has come into bloom this year. Queenlike, she's crowned with a ring of blood-red blossoms. It's early in the day, and cactus wrens are chattering in the giant palo verde tree. It doesn't matter any longer that I will miss Tucson's beauty, this house, this desert, and the women who have become my sisters. It is time for me to go.

August 2, 1993

I am swept up in a flurry of preparations for departure. We must install light fixtures, fix the fountain, and remove the massive fireplace screen and andirons that came from the house I grew up in, along with its original weathervane. Despite the flurry of activity, leaving has become easier over the years.

Painting is on hold. While awaiting my marching orders, I am working on power-mask pieces in my sketch pad. The hard-edged style that suited the anguished emotional transition of previous weeks has softened for the time being; the lightning bolts have abated.

At church yesterday, I wrote on the registration sheet, "We're getting ready to return to Santa Fe. We will be leaving at a moment's notice. Saint Francis in the Foothills has been home to our hearts during our years in Tucson."

August 4, 1993

Eager to tackle a few pages of writing, I've just had Sasha wake Bob up to feed her breakfast—something I hardly ever do. Why not? Perhaps because I write fast, and by the time the family is stirring, I've completed a good portion of my work for the day. But although I've been dutifully taking care of Sasha in the mornings so that Bob could write, it's been months since he's felt like writing; instead, he sleeps in and I resent that I'm *not* sleeping in. Considering this state of affairs, I think it's about time to begin sharing the morning chores.

This afternoon was intriguing. First, I photographed the oil pastels I've been working on these past few months. Photographing artwork places it in an astonishing perspective, allowing the artist to see how much work has been accomplished and how compelling it is. While shooting the pages of my sketchbooks, I could see stories woven throughout three distinct series: the power masks, the woman walking alone in the desert, and the three women at the foot of the mesas. It was these images, combined with daily writing, that led me back to myself after being inundated in grief upon the death of my parents.

Following the photo session, Sasha and I went to the gallery to see my paintings. They looked jewel-like hanging there, but already problems have surfaced. The director wants me to reprice my work by the square inch. "That's how it's done here," she explained. Well, I'd never thought of selling my paintings by the inch! My surprise must have been evident—as well as my concern that the fifty-fifty split with the gallery would make it hard to garner a fair price for the smaller pieces—for Sasha was looking decidedly green. I feared that she might throw up, which would not have boded well for my entering into delicate negotiations. Awkwardly, I asked the director if we could talk next week and scooted out the door with Sasha.

While driving home, I began to mentally calculate the price of a forty-by-fifty-four-inch painting. Partway into the equation I began frothing at the mouth in response to the mental gymnastics. My gallery career in Tucson may well be short-lived, I concluded, recalling the Fool's feather I'd tucked into my belt the day of the gallery lady's visit.

Other aspects of my life in Tucson have born luscious fruit. The women from the Thursday night group are giving me a going-away dinner next week. My work with the creativity support group has also come to a smashing finale. We all seem to have flourished from this "soil preparation" and "seed planting" project. The everyday writing has proved transformative, as has the daily sketchbook drawing.

The greatest reward of my life in Tucson has been finding my lost heart and spirit still rooted in the red dust of New Mexico. After much confusion, I came upon the wise woman in myself. As though listening to a steadily beating drum, I heard her deepest longings: to return to the place that feels like home. Finding that wandering woman is most precious, for now I know what I have to do.

August 13, 1993

Earlier this week I signed the papers on a little house in Santa Fe which, although tiny, has a two-car garage we can cram full with our worldly goods. Since the signing, life has taken on a Castaneda-like quality. My confusion suddenly lifted and I began taking action without a shred of doubt.

Last night I went to the going-away party reeling from exhaustion and exhilaration. I am in the birth canal. My bones have turned soft, my body is stretching, and I am being pushed mightily out of this life and into the next.

Painting holds little interest for me now, and writing is hard to get to. All I can think about is cleaning out closets and getting everything into boxes. Even so, I am continuing with the painting lessons and I try to write. Why? Because these are the tools that guided me to the illumined path out of the dark forest. Like a patient yet insistent mother, I keep leading myself back to the worktable, only to find that the most important work of art is my life!

August 17, 1993

After days of inaction, I am here at the computer expecting all hell to break loose within a few minutes. Kids sense when your attention turns to your own interests, and will intrude with mind-boggling questions. The one I am presently expecting to hear is, "Where are my black leggings with the holes in them?"

To top it off, our little black kitten, Bones, having threaded his way back and forth between my legs, is now marching to and fro on the keyboard. I have to continually push him off, which is distracting—not only to me but to this keyboard prodigy whose little sewing-machine motor is running loudly.

I see a definite connection between "Self-Portrait in Transition," which graces the cover of *Warrior Woman,* and the power-mask painting I recently completed: they are both fierce. "No man would come near her," Laurie said when she saw the power mask.

Nell—a woman whose orbit brings her into my life in its moments of greatest upheaval—noticed the similarity when she came for dinner last night. She was familiar with "Self-Portrait in Transition" because that's what I was painting when she assisted in my departure from Los Angeles. She was the one who set the date, told me where I was going, and called the moving van to come get me. At the time, a four-year relationship was disintegrating, I was losing my studio and home, and I was about to set sail across the desert, eventually to arrive in Santa Fe. I was drooling, starving myself to death, and painting some of the most profoundly disturbing art I've ever produced.

I wonder what sorts of paintings I will produce when I am back in New Mexico, and how well received they will be. Because I invest enormous amounts of energy in each painting, it pleases me when they sell. Yet I am only moderately successful on this front. What matters more are other facets of my existence: that my life is rich, my integrity intact, my emotional accounts clear, and my freedom to paint what I like unobstructed. I've been alcohol free for nearly nineteen years, and I'm devoted to a family I never expected to have. I'm slowly getting my work out into the world: one book is in print, another is ready to hatch, and lots of people own my paintings. Furthermore, I only teach folks I enjoy working with, and I have all the students I want.

Reflecting on my good fortune reminds me that I must call the gallery lady to clear things up. She phoned earlier to say she might need to let go of her newer artists. This warning, together with her request for repricing, suggests that my gallery career in Tucson may indeed be short-lived.

August 19, 1993

Yesterday afternoon I was at my easel when my beloved painting teacher Arnold Schifrin came to mind. "He's in my book," I said to myself, remorseful that I had not notified him. "I must get a copy to him!" Then today, while picking up the mail, I saw an envelope with

Arnold's name in the upper left-hand corner. Tearing it open, I found a sweet note explaining that someone had told him about my book and he'd read it, liked it. That pleases me. The divine hand is piecing together the puzzle of my life.

Aside from that momentary mail break, I've been running through a host of chores like a Tasmanian devil. As it turns out, our little house won't be ready for occupancy until sometime in September, leaving us no choice but to move into the car for the next three to four weeks. We'll be starting this weekend by heading out to Window Rock, Arizona, for a dual speaking engagement at a recovery group: Friday night we'll be at a sweat lodge, Saturday we present, and Sunday we're planning a hike into Canyon de Chelly. From there, we'll continue on to Santa Fe to enroll Sasha in school. As for sleeping arrangements, we'll start out in Pecos at Susan and Lee's house; but if it gets too tight, we'll roll our portable existence somewhere down the road. As usual, there will be no forwarding address.

I've slid into a state of emotional suspension. After all this time of being on hold, we are in motion at the speed of light. I must remember to take the laptop computer, as well as oil pastels, pads, thinner, and my paint-and-brush combo. That way I'll be able to paint between labor pains.

Canyon de Chelly National Monument, Arizona
August 21, 1993

I'm moving agonizingly yet with a heart of joy down the birth canal . . . Our visit here has been beautiful, and the people who invited us, warm and loving, which can almost be expected in circles of recovery.

While I was huddling in the sweat lodge, rivers poured out of me, carrying with them all the dying that has dominated my life these last few years. When it came my turn to speak, I related a dream I once had. In the dream I was looking at a crumbling map that showed Canyon de Chelly with a tiny mark beside it. That speck was Chinle, site of the sweat lodge. As I recounted the dream, I wept. "When I woke up," I said, "I knew I was supposed to come to Canyon de Chelly. It has taken me eight years to get here."

I went on to speak of the joy that arises from being on one's true path, and of the changes wrought by the death of my parents: "My accounts with those two wild people have come full circle. They have moved off to another plane, and now it's time for me to do the same. There is a freedom that comes with the loss of parents, a permission to live whatever sort of life we want to. For me, this freedom—which I consider a gift from my two dear, crazy friends—has paved the way for a return to the land that has become my home." The lodge was filled with sweat, tears, and prayers. An incredible feast followed.

Pecos, New Mexico
August 23, 1993

The trip into Canyon de Chelly was breathtaking. While hiking down with some of the women who had invited us to speak, we were surrounded by soft, swirling rocks. All about us the Mars-red earth stood chiseled into magnificent shapes against the bluest of skies. By the time we reached the White House ruins, I was moved not only by the beauty of the landscape but by its simple holiness. I want to go down into that red opening in the Mother when all tourists are gone and the walls of rock echo silence. I want to look at the night sky and commune with the stars that bear my parents' names.

On the drive east to Pecos, I mentally reviewed the ingredients that activated my healing. For one, I began writing every day, pouring out petty and mundane thoughts as well as the most secret knowings of my heart. Working on yellow legal pads, I gave myself permission to ramble on, to be repetitive, boring, and whiny.

Then, too, there was the daily discipline of sitting down to an empty page in an open sketchbook and using oil pastels, a brush, thinner, and a paint rag. Each day I made at least one drawing. I'd begin by asking myself to make a picture about how I was feeling at that moment. This daily practice birthed some of the most important pieces ever to come through me. Seemingly on their own, the images evolved into three distinct themes—power masks, the woman walking alone in the desert, and the three women conversing at the foot of the mesas—each of which influenced an aspect of my life that needed to heal and grow. As these works were committed to paper, my inner and outer life began to flower.

The third healing ingredient was prayer. Every day, Bob and I made a concerted effort to pray together. One at a time, we would ask out loud where we were supposed to be and what we were supposed to do to be of service; and each new day presented us with an assignment. We also asked to have our fears removed and our attention directed to what God would have us be.

This was the recipe we followed, and having recorded it, I hope to seek it out next time I get lost. Now I am far from lost, for we are going home. We are radiant with happiness, and as joy permeates my life again, I catch glimpses of the free-spirited woman I once was.

We are as settled as can be in Pecos, and I don't care about painting. The river of images that usually flows before my eyes has become glassy, smooth, and opaque. A voice from within me asks, "Will you paint again?" A voice of doom replies, "Artists do their best work when they are not entirely happy. You don't want to get too happy. If you do, your work will suffer." Every turn in the road, it seems, presents new opportunities for a flogging. A lightening of one's mood sets the undertones rumbling: you *can't* be happy, you *can't* have children and be a real artist, you *can't* earn a living making art. Is it any wonder that people fear their creativity?

The truth is I am happy *and* I am an artist. Everywhere I look I see a new wildflower and yearn to peek into its petals, study its little pistils and stamen, get my eye so close up that all I can see is color. I want to wander in the meadows and take trails up the mountains, hypnotized by a stream trickling over shadow-dappled stones as it sings: "All is well. All is in order." I am at peace.

August 27, 1993

I woke up before everyone else, and although I am tired and the mile-high altitude is flattening me, it seemed right to lie quietly in bed and listen to the stirring beneath the surface of my being. Looking at the light filtering through cracks in the shades, I could feel that ten days without a private moment had taken its toll on me. Aware of how hard it is to rouse my creative self when I'm short on quiet time, I decided to turn to women's ancient refuge—the hours when no one else is awake. She-wolves must have solitude!

I wonder who I will be at the end of this transition. We will have a home of our own making in the foothills of the Sangre de Cristos, where I can sink my naked feet into the dusty land, sprinkle my parents' ashes, and let roots I so badly need sink down into the earth. As for the rest of the family, Sasha has suffered from all the upheaval, and so has Bob. He seems to have forgotten how much he needs a home where he can chop wood and tend the fire.

One major change is already under way: Sasha has started kindergarten. Bob and I spent the previous night alternately crying tears of sadness and of joy. Our small, warm bundle once swaddled in a yellow blanket was going off to be "socialized." Sasha herself was anxious about starting kindergarten, but we reminded her that *all* the kids will be new to the pack.

The day we registered her, I recited aloud while filling out the papers, "Sasha Earll—" She interrupted me in an annoyed voice, saying, "I'm *not* Sasha. I'm *Alexandra.*" I was astounded by this proclamation. Reclaiming the name she was given at birth was evidently her way of acknowledging her entry into school as a major passage in her life.

So Sasha is no longer. I am the mother of a kindergartner who wears black leggings she's chewed holes in and black hiking boots. "I look *good* in black," she exclaimed her first day at school. God help us—we've got a prepunk rocker on our hands!

To cope with the massive changes in our lives, we hold a family meeting every morning during the thirty-mile haul from Susan and Lee's house to school. During this meeting, we take turns telling what's going on with us. Bob and I tend to have quite a bit to say; Alexandra likes to listen, but says little. Once, when I asked her teddy bear if *she* would like to share, the bear said she was nervous about starting a new school and excited about making new friends.

After the meeting, we pray together, each taking a turn. Because there is no such thing as censorship in our brand of spirituality, the prayers sound like intimate telephone conversations peppered with colorful language. Alexandra doesn't like to say prayers. She will, however, yell out from the backseat when she cannot hear our words. Listening to intimate messages shared with God seems as good a prayer as any.

While dropping Alexandra off at school yesterday, Bob awakened, as if from a spell. "If you decide to stay on in Pecos," he told me, "I'll go back to clear out the Tucson house." My formerly buried husband is rising from the dead! He knows he wants to come home to New Mexico and is willing to do whatever it takes to make the shift.

I've had nearly an hour to myself and feel much better for it. Great spans of private time are not required to find my way down the ancient crooked stone steps to the caverns where rivers flow. Dreamily, I hear the loud patter of rain on the cottonwoods.

August 31, 1993

To feed the artist who is seeing no images, I'll be visiting a museum today, as well as a few galleries. Something must go in before anything can come out. I expect it will take a while to get my visual machinery up and running now that I am away from the energy of a studio filled with students.

Life is unfolding in a simple and beautiful way. Alexandra is happy with school; her first day there she made a new friend, and now they're stuck together like socks in a dryer. Bob and I are also in a state of delight. After dropping Alexandra off at school yesterday, we drove all the way back to Pecos. Our quiet moments together were punctuated by rolling thunder, and a downpour followed.

In this part of the world we are surrounded by a sea of wildflowers, green pines, and indescribable clouds! Whereas the Arizona skies are dramatic, there is a lofty stature to the clouds that sail across the skies of New Mexico. Everywhere I turn I feel the presence of God. In this bounteous state only one element is missing: I am starving for some classical music, none of which comes on the radio out here in Pecos. I dream about the music of Chopin and plan to track down a cassette of his nocturnes. Listening to great music is vital in the care and feeding of the creative animal.

In all other respects this creative animal is flourishing. Over the weekend Lee, his son Chansce, Bob, Alexandra, and I rode a trail up the nearby mountain. Lee had Chansce tucked in front of him, and Bob had Alexandra. Up we climbed through a forest bursting with butterflies, purple asters, and Indian paintbrush shooting up like flames out of the fresh green grass. After a few hours we stopped in a meadow to dine on apples and cheese. Far below us we could see Susan and Lee's house on the river.

During the descent, I was washed away in a feeling of belonging. For several moments I was one with God. The past year replayed before me—the unsureness and despair, the days of resignation and depression. And then, there I was riding down the mountain, the happiest woman in the Southwest. The hand of God had picked me up by the scruff of the neck and placed me in a niche of the world I had to return to. With my family trailing me down the mountain, all was well, all was in order.

After communing with art in several galleries, I visited a local health club to see about joining. The elegant, dark-eyed woman who showed me around ended the tour with, "I see those cheekbones. What tribe are you from?" I smiled, knowing that although my genealogist had disappeared into the woodwork, I would renew my quest for the woman whose blood pounds in my veins. "We spot each other, you know," she commented. "Yes, I've noticed," I replied, warmed by her remark. To myself I added, "My people are dead. I need to know where I belong. I am drawn to the barely visible trail that leads back through the curtain of time."

Following that quiet encounter in the twilight, I drove north toward Pecos and immediately spotted the full moon "resting" on top of a nearby mesa. As the highway swung northwest, she rolled like a huge luminous globe along the top of the mesa, finally dropping behind Apache Ridge like a ball off a table. A few miles later the road curved northeast, and she rose once again, even more radiant than before. The eerie laughter of Coyote Woman reverberated off the walls of desolate canyons and mesas. There is no doubt in my heart that I am home at last, cradled in the Land of Enchantment.

Index

About the Author

Tina Le Marque is a Santa Fe artist and writer. Her vividly expressionistic oil paintings—drawn from imagery of the Southwest, her emotional life, and her dreams—are archetypal and visionary. Her work is exhibited privately in her mountaintop studio and gallery.

The author's first book in this series, *Warrior Woman,* was published in 1991. She is currently at work on the third book, another intimate look at the inner workings of an artist, writer, and free spirit. A speaker as well, she leads workshops on creativity and personal growth, and is internationally known for her presentations on alcoholism and drug addiction recovery.

When Le Marque is not painting, writing, or conducting workshops, she loves to hike, ride horses, garden, and drape herself in a hammock to read, preferably with her daughter, who is currently a sworn tomboy. She is also learning to fly and play golf, and can often be found at her home or studio amid wild dogs, children, and a river of friends and students.

Order Form

Quantity	Item	Amount
_______	*Warrior Woman: A Journal of My Life As an Artist* ($18.95)	_______
_______	*Coyote Woman: A Continuing Journal of My Life As an Artist* ($18.95)	_______
_______	Coyote Woman poster, 24" x 30" ($40.00)	_______
	Sales tax of 6.25% (for New Mexico residents)	_______
	Shipping and handling (for books, see chart below; for poster, $7.75 each)	_______
	Total amount enclosed	_______

Quantity discounts available

Shipping and handling for books

	Surface	First Class	
United States	$2.70	$4.00	plus $1.00 per book on
Canada	$3.20	$4.20	orders of two or more

Method of payment

❑ Check or money order enclosed (made payable to Artists and Writers Press, in US currency only)

❑ MasterCard

❑ VISA ________-________-________-________

Signature ______________________________ Expiration date ____________

Please photocopy this order form, fill it out, and mail it, together with your name, address, and personal check, money order, or charge-card information, to:

Artists and Writers Press
223 North Guadalupe Street, Suite #303
Santa Fe, NM 87505
800-729-4692